To Mike —

Hummingbirds
in my Hair

Caribbean Adventures of a Diplomatic Wife

With love from
a fellow author

Pamela

Nov 2014

Hummingbirds
in my Hair

Caribbean Adventures of a Diplomatic Wife

....

PAMELA O'CUNEEN

QUARTET

First published in 2014 by Quartet Books Limited
A member of the Namara Group
27 Goodge Street, London W1T 2LD
Copyright © Pamela O'Cuneen 2014
The right of Pamela O'Cuneen to be identified
as the author of this work has been asserted
by her in accordance with the
Copyright, Designs and Patents Act, 1988
A catalogue record for this book
is available from the British Library
ISBN 978 0 7043 7363 1
Typeset by Josh Bryson
Printed and bound in Great Britain by
T J International Ltd, Padstow, Cornwall

Contents

Contents

Foreword

In 1978 I married my prince, KJ, who subsequently metamorphosed into a diplomat. We went together to Africa where we spent sixteen years being astonished, moved, terrified and delighted by Swaziland, Zimbabwe, Angola and surrounding countries. The story of those years was told in my first book, *Culture Shock & Canapés*.

As KJ was an African specialist he was expecting to spend his life among his beloved peoples of the southern African region. But life is not predictable, particularly where international organisations are concerned – and so, after the Rwanda Genocide in 1994, we found ourselves headed for a posting we knew nothing about and could barely find on the map.

This book is the story of six years in the Caribbean region, discovering that the blue sea, sand, rum and palm trees of the package holiday are only a superficial part of the experience, and not necessarily there at all.

We found warm friendship and laughter in a region of rainforest and wildness, where forest-dwellers came to town on a regular basis to raid the local zoo for an easy meal, leaving only the claws of a capybara or a sad bucket of flamingo feathers. We found giant lizards in the garden, caimans in the drains and a multi-coloured choir of birds at dawn. We found shamans in the forest who might claim to speak with spirits of the rainforest or entities from outer space. And above all we found vibrant and colourful societies shot through with a dark, violent and shameful history of slavery and indentured labour, without which the Caribbean as we know it today would not exist.

Like all of life, the story is a mixture of discovery and surprise, delight, fear, and sadness. The Caribbean region is as varied as life itself, and it is invariably in Technicolor. As Gabriel Garcia

Marquez once said, 'Caribbean reality resembles the wildest imagination.'

I salute all the many and varied characters of the book, particularly the wonderful friends and house-helpers whose help and advice made it possible to penetrate the mysteries of a new and different culture. I thank my husband, without whom none of these adventures would ever have happened, my ever supportive mentor, Richard Addis, and the friends, Dutch, Surinamese and Trinidadian, who read the manuscript and made much needed suggestions and corrections.

1

Suri-where? Holland in South America

At a dusty intersection wooden *Hansel and Gretel* houses bordered the roads. A long-dead jaguar skin hung on a tumbledown wooden stall, proud spots splayed like a stiff banner. An anaconda skin and preserved toothy piranhas lay jumbled among rough baskets. Outside the stall ragged boys stood guard over their hopes of instant wealth, two tiny cowering monkeys who hugged each other in a small cage. Nearby a blue and yellow macaw chafed in chains and a woman presided over a stall of knobbly green jackfruit as she tore at a slice of luscious red watermelon with her teeth.

This was Suriname.

We had first heard the name two months before and in the same breath heard it would be our new home.

We knew nothing about this country. Neither, it seemed, did anyone else. Everyone we had asked said 'Suri-where?' It was a mystery country. Did it exist at all? In those days before wide use of the Internet, the largest bookshops in London had no record of it, there were no books about Suriname in the British library system, and tourist agencies in England had never heard of it. No planes from any British airport flew there and there was no Surinamese embassy in London. More and more mysterious. Had we been transferred to somewhere out of *Gulliver's Travels*? Finally I tracked down a Surinamese embassy in Brussels. They sent a brown envelope with a few uninspiring pages of duplicated information, no pictures, no maps, just a few statistics. What sort of place *was* this? And why were we going there?

My husband KJ, a long-time Africa hand, had been left high and dry after the Rwanda genocide. We had been about to take up a position there and were packed and ready to go when the plane containing the president was shot down and the killing commenced. I had no choice but to put our possessions in storage in Swaziland where we were at the time, and to take Star and Magic, our two white English bull terriers, to England where they stayed in quarantine kennels in Dover. There they grew winter coats like two white polar bears while KJ did six months as special envoy to Rwanda, trying to contribute all he could to the task of clearing up the devastation, beginning the restoration of peace and mending the country's shattered infrastructure. In the marketplace of Kigali there were still skulls among the cabbages.

Now months later we were offered a choice of: 'Suriname, Suriname, or Suriname' as our next posting. KJ took the middle one, he said. A southern African specialist, he was, with the usual logic of international organisations, about to leave Africa after thirty-three years for the northern coast of South America. Formerly Dutch Guyana, Suriname nestles between British Guyana and French Guiana.

Why was this isolated Dutch-speaking enclave so unknown to the English-speaking world? We would discover that despite being on the north coast of South America, and very close to the Caribbean, Suriname didn't think it was either South American or Caribbean, but referred back to Holland on all counts. For Surinamers, as we would learn to call them, Holland was the mother country. And, just as for newly 'independent' teenagers, 'mother' can be a love-hate concept, so many Surinamers didn't know quite what they felt about Holland. At one moment Holland was expected to solve all problems and pay all expenses, and at another, Holland was the colonial power, responsible for all ills. Pretty standard in all families and countries, really.

It wasn't as though we were new to the diplomatic game. KJ had been more than thirty years in Africa. Together we had done a sixteen-year stint on that continent and had met the surprises of Swaziland, the king and his courtiers, the game parks, the civil war in Angola, clan conflicts in Somalia and the genocide in Rwanda. Sixteen years on I considered myself immune to the shocks that developing countries could spring and able to see the funny side of most things that happened. I had even written a thesis on culture shock and its effects on families who are constantly transferred around the globe. The story of those early surprises, our reactions, our discoveries and our travels with our beloved pets are told in my first book *Culture Shock and Canapés*.

KJ, who already spoke six languages including fluent Zulu, was now being sent to a continent he had never experienced speaking a language he had never even thought of studying. He was told at HQ that everyone there would speak English and there was no need to learn Dutch. Being KJ, he immediately threw himself into studying the language with one hundred per cent dedication. His room at the Brussels Euro Flats was covered from floor to ceiling with charts of Dutch nouns and verbs. He carried flash cards around in his briefcase for idle moments, and took classes four times a week. As soon as he could, he applied to go on an intensive course in Vught – a renowned language institute in Holland originally founded by an order of Catholic nuns. The nuns were long gone but it was still regarded as one of the best language institutes in Europe.

Back in England I was struggling with the dilemma of what to do about Star and Magic. They had fought in their quarantine kennels in Dover – twice. The first time had been at midnight in the middle of a July thunderstorm. Big white Star, softy that he was, had ended the battle cowering underneath an upturned dog basket. The second fight had taken place in an open field due to over-excitement about some sheep, and they became a snapping, snarling bundle of teeth and fur at the end of two leads. I had lost my nerve when it came to dealing with dogfights. If they fought again they could do each other serious damage and there would be no guarantee that staff in the new posting would be able to cope. We might come back to the house to find an injured or dead dog. One of them would have to go, and it would have to be one-year-old Magic. She was white and dainty and adorable and I loved her dearly but she was younger than Star and not as attached to us. We owed him that loyalty. She was a little princess and needed to be the only dog in a family.

I contacted the Bull Terrier Welfare Society. Joan Kenway, doyenne of Bull Terrierdom, emanated disapproval of anyone who wanted to 'get rid' of a bull terrier. Anxiously I explained that Magic was much loved and to lose her was breaking my heart. There were sheaves of forms to fill in. I put crosses on a diagram of a bull terrier flattened like a bearskin rug to show her markings, described her sweet temperament and her inability to share with another dog, and with one last hug, turned on my heel and left her. Sometimes, even when we do what we know is best, it feels like the worst.

In February KJ received his agrément from the government of Suriname, the agreement from government that an ambassador or Head of Mission has been approved and may take up his post. He left for Paramaribo. We still knew very little about the country. Even encyclopaedias didn't say very much, except that it consisted of ninety per cent rainforest and had a narrow inhabited strip along the coast. The only first-hand information we had was from some Belgian friends from our early expatriate days in Swaziland. They had lived in nearby Curaçao for some years. Their comment was not encouraging: 'Suriname,' they said. 'Mon Dieu! It's as hot as hell and all the people are corrupt.'

We hoped this might be a bit of an exaggeration and decided to reserve judgement. Perhaps our friends had had some bad experiences.

KJ arrived in Suriname's capital Paramaribo at the beginning of March. It was a public holiday and the town was dead. He found himself in a room at the Torarica Hotel, looking out at a wall.

It was hard to form a picture from his descriptions. A lot of wooden houses, he said. Hot, humid, mosquitoes, bright birds, fruit, flowers. He sent photographs of the house and garden inherited from his predecessor. I was largely unimpressed, but entranced by some little palm trees with bright vermillion trunks.

He moved in equipped with borrowed sheets, pots and pans. A friendly housekeeper with the unlikely name of Mabel arrived on her bicycle every morning at 6.30 a.m. and knocked loudly on his window to make sure he was awake. She made fresh fruit juice by hand every morning, he said. He went on a mini-safari into the rainforest by plane and canoe and fell into a river – fortunately the piranhas were off duty.

My departure date was set for 4th May. Having anguished over finding a new home for Magic, I was now deep into arranging Star's transport. He would have to go from Dover to Schiphol airport and on to the KLM plane for Suriname. The kennel owner would drive him to Amsterdam and he would stay in the airport 'Animal Hotel' overnight. There was a minor blip over his measurements. Being irredeemably Anglo-Saxon, I confused inches with centimetres. The forwarding agency phoned and a voice asked: 'Are you transporting a dog or a donkey?'

The tone of voice implied that they would have no problem were it to be a donkey, they just didn't want it to be called a dog.

Departure morning came. As usual, I was travelling with too many suitcases containing all that a fertile imagination suggested might not be available locally. I had packed Earl Grey tea, Scottish oatcakes, and a lifetime supply of Rask dog biscuits. The taxi arrived at 2.30 a.m. This would become a regular drill: catch the first plane out of Heathrow, be in Amsterdam by 7.30 a.m., connect with KLM to Paramaribo. In the next three years, there would never be time for more than one hour's sleep before that alarm went off. Once I overslept and woke to the taxi driver ringing the doorbell.

Schiphol airport is long – very long. The gate for the Suriname flight was at the far end of the airport. When I arrived, I blinked. This was already another country. The area was seething with people, of all physical types, all carrying enormous quantities of luggage and large bags of airport shopping. There were Indian women in saris, prosperous businessmen in dark suits, people wearing what looked like cast-off clothes, people of Chinese origin. Many were staggering under the weight of new TVs, stereo equipment and electrical goods. There were people carrying bundles of rakes and brooms, spades, shovels and tools. It only lacked the chickens and goats. To deal with all this impedimenta a giant rack on wheels stood in the check-in area, already filling up with goods to go in the hold. It was obviously expected that everyone would turn up for this flight over-laden with strange objects. Everyone seemed to know everyone else. The air was full of embraces and greetings. It was a babbling reunion of friends.

The flight was called. I remained landside, at the window, scanning the plane for signs of a dog kennel being loaded. I waited, more anxious by the moment. Was Star on board? That plane was not going until I was sure. Finally, an animal-loving member of ground staff took pity on me and set up terminal-to-ground radio contact with the hold. Yes, Star was on board. He had been loaded first in his own little truck. I agreed to board, crossing my fingers that it was true, and took my seat.

The flight was interminable and noisy. Passengers ran up and down the central aisle, greeted friends, unwrapped and ate spicy snacks, and had parties in the aisle. After a long day, the plane touched down at Zanderij airport. When the door opened, there it was again – memories of our years in Angola – that current of moist, hot air – thick and humid like warm honey on the skin laden with the scent of drains, humanity and unknown spices.

The airport was a vast grey concrete structure, filled with milling small figures, all trying to reunite themselves with vast quantities of baggage. Indecipherable queues were formed, in a babble of Dutch voices. With gratitude I saw KJ and an Indian driver, and was rescued. Then Star in turn had to be rescued from the freight department. We found his cage on the ground in an open concrete area. He was hot and bewildered. Two young men were crouched down peering at him and I heard, not for the last time, that he was a 'pit bull', and a dangerous dog. Poor Star. He never did learn how to be dangerous to anything.

We drove into the city, a distance of forty-five kilometres, along a dusty and potholed road. This was South America but it looked like South East Asia, full of tiny smallholdings, palm trees, bananas, and little peak-roofed thatched houses standing on stilts. There were rice paddies, tropical vegetation and tiny hump-backed buffaloes working in the fields. The route was parched and even the palm trees looked dusty, but closer to the city, houses were built of moulded concrete with elaborate pillars, surrounded by oases of green palms glimpsed over high walls. We drove through a confusion of small, dusty streets edged with terrifyingly deep storm drains. Could it possibly rain *that* much? The centre of town was an entrancing higgle-piggle of decaying wooden colonial houses, built in Dutch style; tumbledown, unpainted, elbows awry and dilapidated. The pointed roofs and tiny windows were straight from *Hansel and Gretel* but the dilapidation and overgrowth suggested the long sleep of the *Sleeping Beauty*.

Instead of going straight to the house KJ introduced me at once to the first of Suriname's bizarre surprises.

'We're not going home,' he said, 'we have to go to a funeral.'

I was hot and sticky off the plane after a long-haul flight. The car stopped outside the old house that served as the EU office. Opposite was a large sandy cemetery. We got out and walked to a small chapel in the grounds. Several hundred people were assembled there to pay tribute to the mother of the Indian Minister for Industry. Her body had been flown home from Holland last night and she was lying in state in her coffin. She was a tiny woman, her smooth-skinned face peeping out from a bed of flowers. We joined the shuffling procession, and solemnly threw flower petals on the coffin to the accompaniment of soft Indian music.

That official and human duty done, the car continued into a dry, sandy suburban area, and drew up outside a house with a wall and a wrought-iron gate. The garden inside was shielded by a sheet of metal. Inside was a concrete path, and a garden of lawn and small shrubs, flowering hibiscus and the red Ixora plant that I would later come to know as 'faya lobi' – 'fire love' or 'passionate love' in the local language.

The house staff were waiting to see this new person they would be working with – a source of as much nervousness to them as to me. We would live in close proximity – three women sharing a kitchen – and our happiness for the next few years would depend on how well we could interact. There would be no escape for any of us during the hours of working together each day. We would learn each other's weaknesses and strengths, make friends where we could, establish boundaries, and learn how to live so that the work could be done with everyone's self respect intact.

These women who would be my friends and helpers in the house were two treasures inherited from my predecessor. Their names were Unasarie Bhoodari (known as Mabel) and Sarinah Issa. Mabel shook our hands strongly and Sarinah gave a shy little bob. There was a chorus of: 'Good morning Mevrouw, Good Morning Mijnheer!'

Mabel, who had black, wavy hair and smiling eyes, was a solid stocky lady from Guyana, of Hindustani and African descent. She was direct in her opinions and expressed them in a mixture of English, Dutch, and the local patois, which used to be called 'Taki Taki' ('Talk Talk') but was now more politely known as Sranaan Tongo (Suriname tongue). She frequently used all three languages in the same sentence. KJ immediately nicknamed Mabel 'the sergeant major'. She had a habit of giving us permission to do things in our own house!

'You can do that Mevrouw!'

Javanese Sarinah, (nickname 'the mouse') was tiny, quiet, patient and saintly. She had to be, because Mabel ordered her everywhere. Whatever I said would be passed down the line in stentorian tones, in a comic double act.

'Mabel, the birds have made a mess on the front veranda!' I would remark.

Immediately 'Sarinah! Get the brush and dustpan!' would ring out down the corridor, and little Sarinah would come scurrying. We very soon discovered that Mabel was one of the earth's most generous, kind and warm-hearted people, and that Sarinah, far from disliking her subordinate role, preferred to be directed, and was lost without her benevolent 'sergeant major'. They were the greatest of friends. Even their birthdays were on the same day.

Mabel had serious shopping skills and a bicycle. She loved to get up very early, when it was cool, to go to the market. When she arrived at the house by 6.30, she, her bicycle, its handlebars and saddlebags, were hung around with beans, bananas, eggs, chickens, and an astonishing array of vegetables, which she piled up triumphantly on the kitchen table for my admiration.

And the vegetables really were astounding. One of the first surprises was 'kouseband' (pronounced 'korsebahn'), which I thought must translate as 'coarse beans', which they are. Big green beans a metre long. But the word means a garter, who knows why. But it was not until I saw the 'poe' that my eyes really stood out on stalks. 'Poe' (pronounced 'poo') is a green marrow that can grow to a metre long, but in shapes of giant genitalia that should be censored. We were highly diverted the first time we read 'roast poe' on the in-flight menu of Air Suriname. We just had to try it. And I still have a recipe for 'poe cake', which causes uncontrollable giggles among the under-fives.

Mabel and Sarinah cooked scrumptious and hugely calorific local foods. Sarinah's specialities were South East Asian dishes such as Nasi Goreng and Bami Goreng. Mabel often made Saoto Soup (soto means soup in Maleisch, the old Indonesian language). The corners of the fridge were stuffed with mysterious little packets of spices, seeds, dried leaves and assorted condiments. Occasionally they announced that they were 'doing a surprise' for lunch and I was not allowed into the kitchen for the morning. The surprise would be brought to the table with triumph, and the ladies would hover with expectation on their faces as we tried the first mouthfuls.

There were crispy little fried spring rolls called 'lumpia', and vegetable roti which Mabel would make on the stove, allowing the dough to rise up like a football on the hotplate before she beat it into submission and it collapsed into delicious hot, flaky layers. On one rather difficult day the 'surprise' was 'coconut and cow-meat', the 'cow-meat' so tough that even Star under the table was defeated.

After a month I wrote to a friend:

So what is Suriname like? It is called the 'Land of Seven Peoples'. There are Amerindian, Creole, 'Bos Negers' (the local name, which sounds highly politically incorrect to non-Surinamers, means Bush Negroes), Chinese, Indian (called Hindustani), Javanese, and Dutch people all living together in harmony. There are also other racial groups – all relics of a history which is difficult to fathom, but is slowly re-

vealing itself. It is a small country which has been colonised by British, French and Dutch in the past. Which results in a few contradictions – for instance we drive on the left, but use left-hand-drive vehicles imported from America. This means that we all drive blind, with no idea if anyone is planning to overtake. Fortunately, if they do it is usually very slowly. So far I have not dared to drive anywhere, since the roads are full of potholes, and deep, deep storm drains. There are very few names on the streets, but in any case there seem to be no urban maps available in the shops.

This was the Caribbean, but contrary to general fantasies, there were neither blue oceans nor golden sands although there were plenty of waving palm trees of different species. Due to some unfortunate design miscalculation, the Amazon emptied its mud into the ocean in the coastal area north of Paramaribo, so there were no recognisable beaches, just a shifting area of mud flats and mangrove trees between the town and the coast, inhabited by millions of mosquitoes, manatees, and at certain seasons giant turtles who came to lay their eggs. It was also the site of the Hindustani cremation ground.

Closer to home it was a city like no other I had ever seen. When the first settlers arrived, they came with ideas of European architecture in their memories and set about reproducing those designs in wood. The old buildings were still stubbornly standing, albeit with difficulty, and it was easy to go back in time and imagine the clip-clop of horses and carriages along the streets. The houses were built with Dutch gables and sloping roofs, and the city boasted 'the largest wooden cathedral in the southern hemisphere', a huge yellow-painted gothic edifice. The Presidential Palace must once have been very grand, and had recently been repainted green and white in honour of Suriname's twentieth year of independence. Among the city buildings were the moons, stars and minarets of 'the largest wooden mosque in the southern hemisphere', which stood next to 'the largest wooden synagogue in the southern hemisphere', built in massive baroque style. These two cultures and religions, Judaism and Islam, warring elsewhere in the world, here had their places of worship standing side by side on one piece of ground with no fence between. And Paramaribo seemed to have 'the largest number of unfinished Hindu temples in the southern hemisphere' as well. There were several in suburban areas, obviously destined for great grandeur, all domed and arched and decorated with twisted and fluted pillars and all apparently frozen in time until someone came up with enough money to build the next section.

Shops abounded, some relatively large in 1950s style, some tiny and jumbled, all of them influenced by the early days when all traders in the colony were general dealers. Birdcages and pencils stood side by side with plastic hair slides, rocking chairs, buckets, lipsticks and the ubiquitous Coca-Cola.

My first attempt at shopping took me into a city shop. It was large, concrete and grey and Eastern European in feeling. I needed electric plugs. It involved endless queuing at barred and barricaded booths marked 'Kassa'. There was much scurrying about to different windows with little tickets and receipts before the goods could be taken away. Having spotted the plug, I had to beg for it in Dutch at a forbidding barred window, fill out a form, stand on one leg at another window, pay at yet another, have the form stamped, and wait again. Finally a glum-looking employee emerged from the middle distance, bearing the object I hardly even wanted any longer.

Other shops, like supermarkets of the 1950s, stocked a delightful muddle of Dutch butter and cheese (always Edam or Gouda), Indian, Chinese and Indonesian spices and condiments, Kerrygold powdered milk (why?) and quite a lot of tins and bottles with mysteriously scratched-out sell-by dates. All the supermarkets smelled of the same strange combination of old cheese, drains and ancient vegetables and I had a suspicion that at night they might be transformed into rats' ballrooms.

One small shop that fascinated us was best seen at night. We spotted it, brightly illuminated one evening when we were driving down Gravenstraat. People were strolling past, pointing and window-shopping with great interest. It was a coffin shop – beautiful caskets in all sizes and colours of satin lining, neatly displayed on shelves like books in a library for the enthusiastic window-shoppers to make their choice.

Markets were piled high with watermelons, red, pink and yellow, mangoes, papayas and the 'pompelmoes', gigantic pink grapefruit up to ten inches in diameter – one segment made a meal. There were bunches of the metre-long korsebahn green beans tied together with string, extravagant piles of coconuts and huge yellow passion fruit, green curly poe, purple toffee-fruit, and shiny, angular yellow carambola or star fruit.

Flower sellers loaded up little pickup trucks and sold their array of tropical splendour in the shade by the Torarica Hotel. There were plastic buckets of waxy anthuriums, in every shade of red and salmon and creamy white shaded with green, great red and green parrot beak heliconias, which grew wild in the jungle, and armfuls of orchids, bizarrely shaped and speckled. Friendly, smiling Javanese vendors plied scissors, ribbons and cellophane paper with nimble fingers and produced instant miracles of flower arrangement, each bouquet presented with courteous deft perfection.

Together with the flowers and fruit, the birds were life enhancing. Suriname boasted six hundred and twenty species, and a large number of these sang in the garden every morning. The dawn chorus was a revelation. Like a Bach fugue it began with one early voice and others joined in one by one, until they were weaving an orchestra of sound. And the sweetest, loudest and longest song was sung by an ordinary little speckled brown bird called a tree creeper, who sat on a telephone wire suspended above the house dustbins, singing his heart out.

Soon after I arrived, on 9th May, it was Europe Day again. This time it would be held in the Torarica Hotel's reception room. The office had a holiday in honour of the day and we were at home. It was very quiet. There was a ring at the gate. It was a florist delivering a vast bouquet of flowers from the Indonesian embassy backed by a geometrical structure made of split and woven palm leaves. Another ring, and an equally large arrangement arrived from the French embassy. This went on all day. The house was crammed with floral congratulations and good wishes. We were running out of space to put them. It was our first introduction to the Surinamers' love of flowers. Flowers were obviously one of the national languages. They were given at every opportunity – for birthdays, funerals and anniversaries, for national days, for the opening of a new shop, for religious festivals and on any other occasion. Embassies sent flowers to other embassies, businessmen sent flowers to other businessmen, and women gave flowers to their friends. It was charming and graceful and the arrangements were awe-inspiring in their tropical splendour and artistry.

That first Europe Day function went well. KJ did his speech about the foundation of the European Union, with its aims of 'Never Again War!' and 'Never Again Hunger!' He had done it in Portuguese, in Siswati and now – at least that part of it – in Nederlands. He was momentarily stymied for the word for war, and President Venetiaan supplied the phrase from the audience: 'Nooit meer oorlog.'

Life in Paramaribo felt cut off from the rest of the world. It was always the same. In the first weeks of a new diplomatic posting, one is cloistered behind a wall with staff who are still strangers, without friends, and in those days separated from familiar voices by the cost of long-distance phone calls.

The one phone call I did make was to the Bull Terrier Welfare Society in England. Had Magic found a new home? 'Oh,' said a distant voice. 'Didn't we let you know? She has found the perfect home.'

She was living a new life with a loving family, with her very own eleven-year-old girl to play with, her own couch, and her own little sleeping bag for camping holidays. And she even had a new surname. She was now Magic Love. Photographs were sent. She was happy, it seemed. And if she was happy, in this respect at least, so was I.

But she was in England. This was Paramaribo. Here the language was Dutch, or Nederlands, as I would learn to call it. Unsurprisingly, local newspapers were in Nederlands, the radio and TV news were in Nederlands, posters on walls announcing forthcoming events were in Nederlands as were labels on goods in the shops.

I felt dim and stupid when I went out – more so than in Zimbabwe or Swaziland, where English was the *lingua franca*, and more so than in Angola, where we managed pretty well in Portuguese. Here, despite an impressive ninety-five per cent literacy rate in the country, and the confident predictions from HQ that English was spoken, there were large numbers of people who not only did not speak any English (why should they?) but did not speak Nederlands either. Sarinah, our talented cook, spoke the old Javanese of her ancestors, and a little Sranaan Tongo, with minimal Nederlands. Marmin, the tall Javanese gardener, spoke no Nederlands at all. We communicated by sign language. My digging and clipping gestures improved daily. And sellers in the markets were likely to be limited to Sranaan Tongo only. Thank heavens for Mabel who could bargain in English, Sranaan Tongo and Nederlands all at the same time.

So why not learn to speak Nederlands? The first reason for not taking lessons had been that assurance that it would not be necessary.

'Everyone speaks English,' KJ had been told.

This was true to some extent. All Dutch people from Holland and many Surinamers spoke English more than adequately for most social occasions. But it soon became apparent that when the conversation became *really* interesting, or complex or philosophical, the Dutch and Surinamers would enthusiastically close ranks and shift back into Nederlands without compunction. This national characteristic left us high and dry, standing as outsiders on the outskirts of some fascinating discussions. I began to look around for language lessons. There had been a language school, but it had closed: 'Because everybody can speak Nederlands there is no need!'

'Oh yes there is!' I thought.

There was one highly trained tutor called Patricia, a superb teacher and linguistics graduate. Classes with her were a joy but a severe strain on the budget. I went to lessons and learned strings of verbs, and a lot of interesting facts, but somehow they never quite solidified into a language.

In the early weeks life revolved around the house, with a few evening work functions to attend. During the day I kept moving.

Mabel and Sarinah were enthusiastic cleaners and went through the entire house assiduously every single day, no matter what I said. If Star and I stood still too long we were in danger of the cobweb brush. To escape this frenzy of cleanliness I would put on a hat and risk the humid heat for a walk around the garden with Star. Outside the front gate we sometimes saw some creatures grazing, baked in the heat. Theoretically they were probably sheep, but they resembled no sheep any Australian had ever seen. Small, thin, dirty grey in colour, wool-less and spindly, I mentally christened them 'shoats', since they looked like nothing so much as a sheep-goat hybrid. It was hard to imagine that they would yield either wool or meat. The heat in Suriname was intense so why would they grow a thick coat?

There was something about the combination of heat and high humidity that heated up the blood and the bones. After a short walk outside I would be boiling internally and in need of yet another shower.

Star and I would walk around the house, all the way to the dustbins, re-examining the plants and trees en route. And there were many to examine – multicoloured hibiscus, red, pink and yellow faya lobi, red and orange heliconias, and purple-flowered creeper flooding over the fences. There was a carambola or star fruit tree. Mabel made a sour-sweet yellow juice from the fruit but it was not kind to its namesake, Star, since there was a colony of red fire ants who lived on the ground below the tree. One hot afternoon Star and I stepped simultaneously into the milling river of ants and fled, our feet and legs bursting into flames. Star kept running on the principle that if he ran fast enough, perhaps he could outrun the pain. On his third circuit of the garden I brought him down with a rugby tackle and we both sat with our feet in cold water prior to a liberal application of camomile lotion. We took care that it only happened once.

There were self-sown papaya trees, and a Caribbean cherry – bright red segmented fruits with a stone, reputed to have the highest vitamin C content of any fruit in the region. They were juicy, acidic and tart. I ate the high ones while Star nibbled at those on his level. We had a cinnamon tree, its bark begging to be furled off into cinnamon sticks, and just outside the kitchen there was a pomerac tree like a huge hollow cathedral. Standing with my head inside the low branches I could look up at rows of bright pink-purple fruit, like tiny cerise pears. The blossom was the same bright psychedelic pink and its pom-poms made a fluffy carpet on the ground. If I was very still and quiet, tiny green and purple hummingbirds with wings like shot silk would whirr past my ears, fanning my hair in their quest for the sugary fruit.

Back inside, I would spray and water the indoor plants, and retire to the study while the relentless cleaning went on. The BBC in those early days was a great blessing. Never before had I been so reliant on it, but I discovered that the World Service repeated programmes endlessly during the week. The same episode of *The Hitchhiker's Guide to the Galaxy* palled the third time round. I became a lady who did needlework, and started on petit-point tapestry. I sat there for hours. One day when KJ came home for lunch he asked what I had been doing.

'Waiting for the year 2001!' I said. 'When you retire!' Sometimes a new posting can feel like that. What was the point of it all?

On the other hand, repetitive or not, the BBC could sometimes provide diversion. Sometimes names were not very clear. On one news bulletin a brother of Prince Noradong Sianhouk of Cambodia featured. But could he really have been called Prince Noradong *Sillyboot*? And there was that chap who seemed to be called Crapchook. Listen as I might I could not make out any more likely name. On the other hand, some names are just unfortunate to the English ear. We used to get letters from a lady official at HQ called Frau Schittekat.

The mornings were long. Because of the heat, government office hours were from 7 a.m. until 2 p.m., with no break for lunch. There was no point working when no one else was available, so all other offices conformed. But it was a long and hungry time between 7 a.m. and 2 p.m. In the beginning we all starved. KJ took 'play lunch' to the office. Just to stay alive.

In the evenings there were work cocktails and functions to attend. I described them to a friend in this depressed and jaded period. 'There are evenings when there is a function to celebrate a national day or similar festivity. You know the unvarying routine: best dress, comfortable but elegant shoes, rhubarb rhubarb for half an hour, silence, totally unintelligible speech in either a foreign language or an accent that is so heavy it might as well be, a toast, unintelligible reply, toast, followed by trays of the ubiquitous stuffed eggs, meatballs and samosas.' It seems that I was really unimpressed at the time.

Then it hit me. What was happening? In Zimbabwe, five years ago, I had written a dissertation on the topic of culture shock. Here it was hitting in its full-blown form and I was in danger of not recognising it. This was the dislocation of moving to a new country, the loss of all the externals of life, particularly the familiar, comforting and pleasant ones, the depression and alienation that is almost bound to set in some time during the first six months. After the initial honeymoon period in a new culture where everything is interesting and fascinating, most sojourners experience culture shock to some degree. It is much studied and well documented and can manifest as depression, irritation, nervousness of unfamiliar surroundings, fears about hygiene, mild ill health, or intense homesickness. We mostly fail to recognise the symptoms and only realise that we have not been functioning well until our sense of humour kicks in again after six months to a year.

It would take a lot of smiling, a lot of pretending to be positive and efforts to be proactive before things would change. And it would take time. I had studied the condition, written articles about it, given talks and lectures on it. However well warned and prepared we are, it always takes us by surprise. Now that I had seen what was happening perhaps it would be easier to get on with life rather than spending time morosely stabbing canvas with a tapestry needle and listening to repeated programmes of the BBC.

So what was there to do in the town? People were said to play tennis – somewhere – but in this heat and humidity? There were apparently trips to the rainforest, of the push-your-own-canoe-through-the-piranhas variety. The one sheet of information we managed to find about the country said: 'Tourism is undeveloped.

17

Travellers outside Paramaribo are advised to take their own hammock and food.'

KJ and I sometimes went to the Torarica Hotel on a Saturday morning for coffee. The coffee shop was dark and empty, and the cakes, although they looked delicious, all had a curious taste of Lysol. There were a couple of cinemas, which showed things like *King Fu* in Dutch. There was a Nederlands bookshop and video shops. Being a multiracial society there were Chinese restaurants, and a large number of tiny basic cafés with cement floors and iron tables. There were roti shops, which I never dared to enter, though they smelled delicious, and the Bali, which had spicy South East Asian rijstafel and pretty cane furniture. There was the Hofstede, with its exquisite flower murals and 'International Cuisine'. But surely life should be about more than eating out!

It was diplomatic to disguise any lack of enthusiasm for the new posting. Local residents had a habit of fronting up at social functions and saying brightly: 'Don't you love our beautiful Suriname?' It was difficult to find a reply that was honest and acceptable at the same time. The best I could do was to talk diplomatically about the flowers and birds. At least I had seen some of those in the garden, whereas the little else I had seen so far was decidedly unpromising.

The government chief of protocol was a young woman. She had recently been promoted and was very enthusiastic. Unusually, she came to the airport to welcome us to the country saying: 'Don't you love…!' A few days later an invitation arrived to a ladies' coffee morning. There I met the ladies of the department and the other wives. It was a pleasant morning. A speech of welcome was made, and I was presented with a gift – a book about the orchids of Suriname. At the conclusion of the speech the lady protocol officer made the memorable remark: 'This welcome gathering is one of our traditions. I invented it!'

It sounds as though there should have been no reason for feeling so alienated, depressed and directionless in these early weeks. But as I should have realised from my own studies, people who are constantly transferred to different countries suffer more stress than they know. For us there had been a lot of changes in recent years

– Somalia, Rwanda, losing the pets, leaving our beloved Swaziland and all our friends, KJ's time in Brussels, leaving England again, adjusting – or not adjusting – to Suriname. According to studies of life stress factors, such accumulated stress can lead to illness within two years.

And so in December we both fell ill with a bad flu. KJ came down with it in the middle of a conference in Trinidad. It hit me at the end of a day when I had given a talk to a new intake of Peace Corps volunteers at a stifling hot centre some miles outside Paramaribo and had then spent five hours face-painting tiny children at the Diplomatic Ladies' International Bazaar. The illnesses lasted a month, and turned into lung infections and pneumonia. KJ had dengue fever as well. In the process we found out a lot more than we ever wanted to know about the health service – or lack of it – in Suriname. The doctors were highly trained, pleasant and efficient, when we could get in to see them. But it entailed hours of waiting in hospital anterooms, sitting on wooden benches for three hours at a time, together with queues of two hundred sick Surinamers. We felt ill enough, but most of our fellow patients were far more seriously ill and coping in far poorer conditions. The support staff were far from helpful – hostile, even. It seemed as if we, the patients, were interfering with their lives. Antibiotics were finally prescribed. X-rays were taken and tests for TB were done. Who knows exactly what we had – after fifteen years – no test results have ever appeared. But eventually, thanks more to the passing of time than to any medical help, we recovered.

While that was all happening I had a birthday. We were directed to Max Chin a Sen's jewellery store in town to look for a present. A set of gold bracelets was chosen. There were seven of them in the set, each incised with a different pattern, symbolising the seven peoples of Suriname. Standing inside the Aladdin's cave of jewellery was a huge vase, waist-high. Towering red, green and pink heliconias were in the vase, flowing down in undulating waves. I forgot the jewellery for the moment. The proprietor Max Chin a Sen, was delighted with my delight.

'Would you like some flowers?' he asked.

'That would be lovely,' I replied politely, anticipating a small bunch of something.

The next morning there was a ring at the gate. As in *Macbeth*, Birnam Wood had apparently come to Dunsinane. There appeared to be a waving forest outside the wall, waiting to come in. When the gate opened, the forest moved along the path to the front door, propelled by a pair of canvas-clad feet. It was Max's gardener, from down the road. Max was a collector. He collected heliconias of all kinds and colours, from South and Central America and Hawaii, and his garden was a small tropical forest. Enough flowers to create a small indoor forest came in the front gate, on stems that were seven feet high. The largest bouquet anyone could ever receive.

Life during the first months in Paramaribo had been bounded by the four walls of the house and garden. Halfway through the year KJ heard of a small car that was being sold second-hand by a secretary from the French embassy. It was a Japanese car, apparently made for extremely small Japanese people. I had to fold myself into uncomfortable shapes to get in and entrance to the back seat was impossible without jackknifing at every joint. It had been stuck at the port for some time before delivery, and everything shiny or in any way detachable had been removed, including the radio, but apart from that, it was in good condition with a very low mileage.

The only trouble was that despite having driven since the age of seventeen, here in Suriname I was too nervous to try. Paramaribo was laid out in a network of streets and drainage canals, with the occasional 'sluis' – a wide storm drain six feet deep to trap the unwary reverser. In addition, although the streets presumably *had* names, most of the time the names were not on the streets, or they might be at one end of the road and not at the other. People seemed to drive by intuition. After cowering for several months, I had to regain some self-respect as a driver. It was a Saturday afternoon. I took my courage and the car keys and set off without a map, since there were none.

'At least,' I thought, 'I can turn left at the corner, go up the main Commeweinestraat and come back round the block. Can't get lost doing that. It won't take long and then I'll have a cup of tea to recover.'

I set out, in the little left-hand-drive car, driving on the left. There were cars hot on my tail, hooting and passing on the blind side. I turned right in a panic and found myself in lands unknown to man. The streets were full of lakes from recent rain, they twisted in crescents and at odd angles. I had no idea where home was. There was no point stopping to ask directions, since my Nederlands was so minimal as to be non-existent. The only people I saw shouted at me. I was probably going the wrong way round some sacred roundabout. It seemed to go on for hours. What would I do if night fell? Panic set in. I might never get home. Ever! It was the stuff of nightmares. I crossed another main road and found myself careening up a track leading into a field. Glory be! It was the Zorg en Hoop commercial airport not far from home. Sweating, I circled round, and scooted out of the airfield hoping no one had seen me on the runway. I was approaching home from the other end of the street. I put the car away and fell out of it with relief, vowing never again to drive in this benighted place.

It might have remained that way, had it not been for the American Marines and St Patrick. The small group of Marines attached to the US embassy were celebrating St Patrick's Day. They had decorated their house with truly American thoroughness. Everything was green that could be greened. There was green beer, there were green drinks, green rice with the food and American-Irish music playing over the loudspeakers. I had been invited to bring the Celtic harp and sing Irish folk songs – dressed in green of course. KJ was approached by a smiling young woman – in green – who said in an Australian accent: 'I'm Patsy Maloney and I heard there was a real Irishman here. I want to meet you.'

Patsy and her husband Claude came from my home town, Perth. We shared an alma mater. We sat on a concrete step and talked about home. They were part of a group of young Australian engineers working in the bauxite industry and they were enthu-siastically Australian. Inspired by the St Patrick's night, and the concept of national days, they would organise an Anzac Day party later in the year. Would we come?

For the Anzac Day party the young people had listed everything that was most Australian. They would have Australian beer, Australian flags, kangaroos in all the forms they could muster, Vegemite sandwiches, meat pies, Anzac biscuits and Lamington cakes (sponge cake covered with chocolate icing and desiccated coconut). The men would teach the Surinamers to play two-up, and all those who could, should wear 'something Australian'. I brushed down my Akubra hat, and KJ found an equivalent. It was a good party, albeit confusing for the Surinamers. The facial expressions of elegant Indian ladies as they bit into a Vegemite sandwich made the whole event worthwhile.

Patsy phoned a few days later. There were some good photos. Would I come to see them one afternoon? Rashly I agreed. But I would have to drive. That vow would have to be broken. And so thanks to St Patrick's night and the Anzac party I set out to find Patsy's house in Krakalaan. Up Commeweinestraat again, turn right at the white house, along three streets, past a bar with the jaw-dropping and unforgettable name of Shitan Snack, then right again. I committed the route to memory. Now there was one place I could drive to. The door to freedom was open.

Patsy and the Australians became part of life. As usual in difficult postings, everyone shared their talents. A mathematician by profession, Patsy coached me in computing. And in return came to a meditation group in my house to help her to relax. Her sewing and coffee mornings became a legendary support group for young expat women who were new and bewildered in Paramaribo. And the Australians decided to hold a Melbourne Cup lunch party.

This slightly tongue-in-cheek event was to be held, due to the time difference, after the running of the race since there was little danger of anyone in Suriname knowing who had won. Hats would be de rigueur – the more inventive the better. One young South African woman wore the lid of her laundry basket decorated with faya lobi flowers. This time the cuisine was not confined to Australian specialities (though Aussies do a great deal more than meat pies and Vegemite sandwiches). The high points of the lunch would be the hat competition, and the sweepstake.

After horse numbers were issued we listened to the race. It had been pre-recorded over someone's answering machine, and so was even more gabbled and incomprehensible than race commentaries usually are. Fortunately the results had been sent from Australia by fax or they would have remained a mystery forever. The winners collected their prizes with bemused expressions on their faces wondering why they were being given small amounts of money. It all left the local guests, elegant Hindustani and Chinese young woman, looking very puzzled indeed. The Hindustanis understood the gambling but were not sure whether they should be involved and the Chinese liked the idea of gambling but couldn't work out what they had gambled on or why they won, and everyone looked very sceptically at the flower bedecked laundry basket lid.

As the end of the year approached, we discovered that New Year is the Big Celebration in Suriname. It begins in November when the first fireworks go off (just practising) and goes on until Chinese New Year. Children buy little bunches of red Chinese fire-crackers called 'pagaras' and explode them in the streets, or throw them around. Mabel called them 'bombels' as in: 'De little bombels, so noisy, I near to fall off de bicycle!'

Sometimes, at parties they were let off in long, long strings. The first time we heard a string of pagaras exploding we were in the front garden. Our hearts beat faster as we thought there had been a coup, or that an entire ammunition dump had gone up, somewhere in town, and we waited with trepidation to hear what had happened. It was only later that we discovered that what we had heard was just a favourite party activity. Sometimes, on a Sunday morning whole streets would apparently be covered with red 'rose petals' – the red papers from pagaras. The bangs started every morning before it was light, and went on until after midnight. It was wearing. Star came in hurriedly from the garden when the noises happened. I worried that the children from the school next door might throw a cracker at him through the hedge. It was all preparation for New Year's Eve when, we were told, everyone let off fireworks, and the whole town smelt of gunpowder for days.

Christmas came. We still had little energy after our flu. It was a quiet time except for the incessant bombels. Neither Christmas decorations nor trees were to be found in the shops that year. But there was a palm tree in the garden – the one with the bright red trunk. It had red fruit that the birds loved, and branchy antlers. We harvested the branches, I sprayed them gold and hung them with our few minuscule Christmas baubles, and some Christmas lights. It made an exquisite little tree. I had wondered if we would be reduced to roast parrot or roast macaw but found a piece of turkey at the last moment. So resolutely traditional in the tropics, we had our tree, our modest turkey, a bit of Christmas pudding and in the old spirit of colonial adventurers we toasted each other. 'Can't let the standards slip, old chap!'

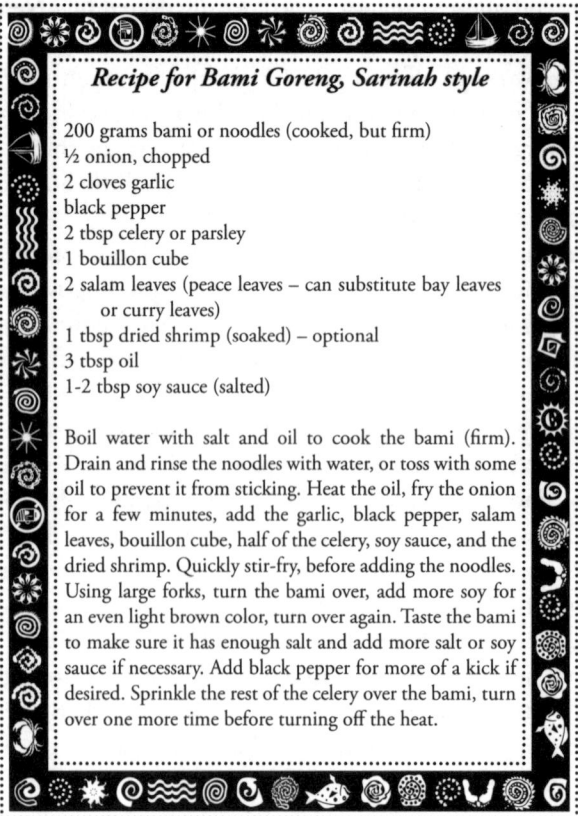

Recipe for Bami Goreng, Sarinah style

200 grams bami or noodles (cooked, but firm)
½ onion, chopped
2 cloves garlic
black pepper
2 tbsp celery or parsley
1 bouillon cube
2 salam leaves (peace leaves – can substitute bay leaves
    or curry leaves)
1 tbsp dried shrimp (soaked) – optional
3 tbsp oil
1-2 tbsp soy sauce (salted)

Boil water with salt and oil to cook the bami (firm). Drain and rinse the noodles with water, or toss with some oil to prevent it from sticking. Heat the oil, fry the onion for a few minutes, add the garlic, black pepper, salam leaves, bouillon cube, half of the celery, soy sauce, and the dried shrimp. Quickly stir-fry, before adding the noodles. Using large forks, turn the bami over, add more soy for an even light brown color, turn over again. Taste the bami to make sure it has enough salt and add more salt or soy sauce if necessary. Add black pepper for more of a kick if desired. Sprinkle the rest of the celery over the bami, turn over one more time before turning off the heat.

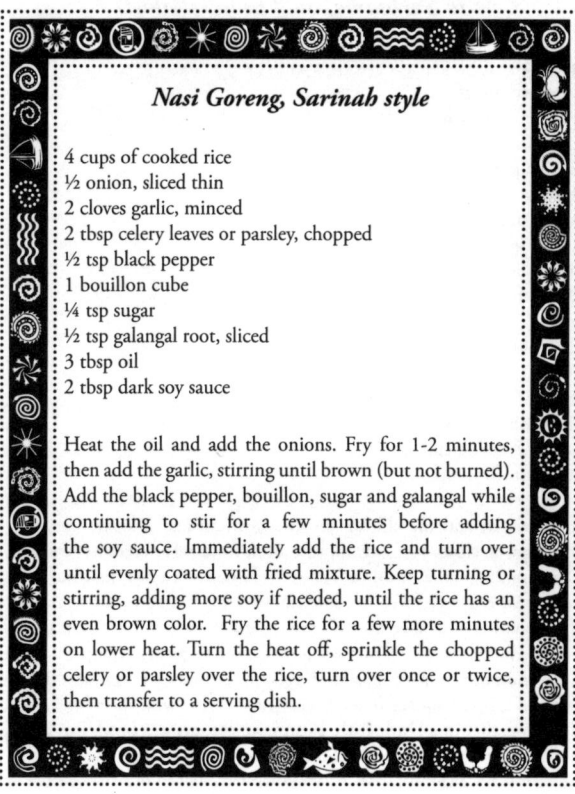

Nasi Goreng, Sarinah style

4 cups of cooked rice
½ onion, sliced thin
2 cloves garlic, minced
2 tbsp celery leaves or parsley, chopped
½ tsp black pepper
1 bouillon cube
¼ tsp sugar
½ tsp galangal root, sliced
3 tbsp oil
2 tbsp dark soy sauce

Heat the oil and add the onions. Fry for 1-2 minutes, then add the garlic, stirring until brown (but not burned). Add the black pepper, bouillon, sugar and galangal while continuing to stir for a few minutes before adding the soy sauce. Immediately add the rice and turn over until evenly coated with fried mixture. Keep turning or stirring, adding more soy if needed, until the rice has an even brown color. Fry the rice for a few more minutes on lower heat. Turn the heat off, sprinkle the chopped celery or parsley over the rice, turn over once or twice, then transfer to a serving dish.

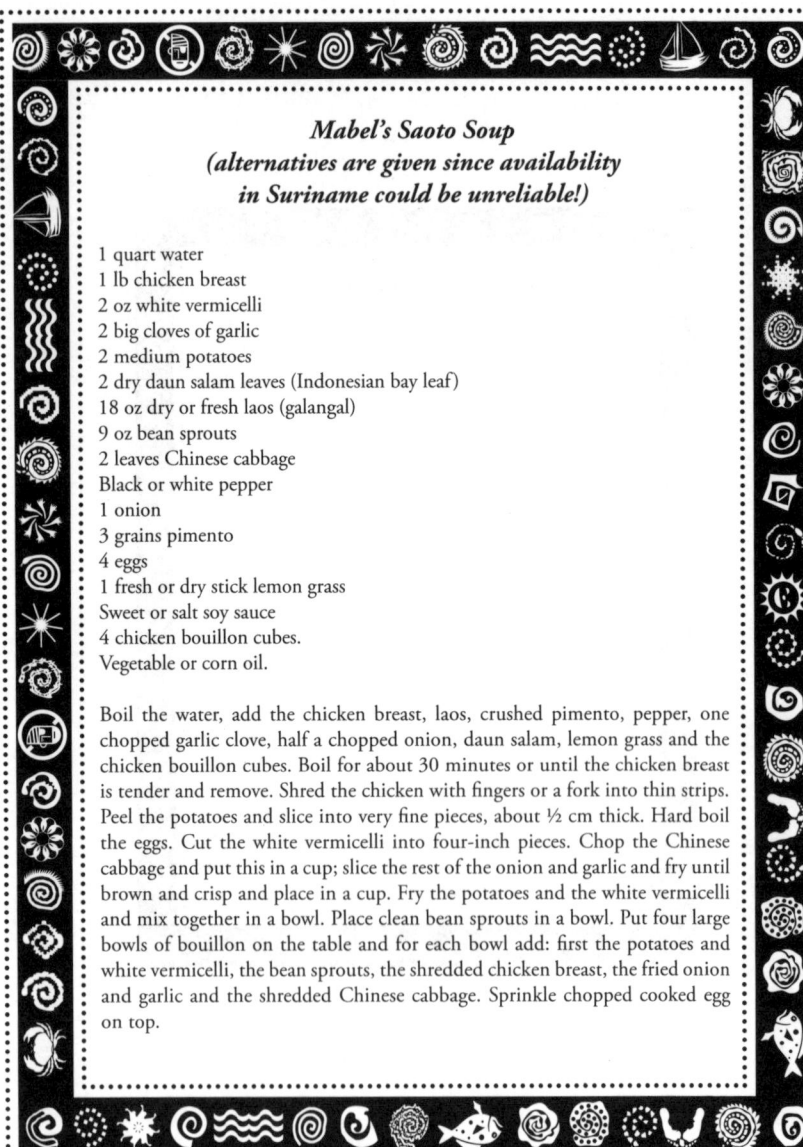

Mabel's Saoto Soup
(alternatives are given since availability
in Suriname could be unreliable!)

1 quart water
1 lb chicken breast
2 oz white vermicelli
2 big cloves of garlic
2 medium potatoes
2 dry daun salam leaves (Indonesian bay leaf)
18 oz dry or fresh laos (galangal)
9 oz bean sprouts
2 leaves Chinese cabbage
Black or white pepper
1 onion
3 grains pimento
4 eggs
1 fresh or dry stick lemon grass
Sweet or salt soy sauce
4 chicken bouillon cubes.
Vegetable or corn oil.

Boil the water, add the chicken breast, laos, crushed pimento, pepper, one chopped garlic clove, half a chopped onion, daun salam, lemon grass and the chicken bouillon cubes. Boil for about 30 minutes or until the chicken breast is tender and remove. Shred the chicken with fingers or a fork into thin strips. Peel the potatoes and slice into very fine pieces, about ½ cm thick. Hard boil the eggs. Cut the white vermicelli into four-inch pieces. Chop the Chinese cabbage and put this in a cup; slice the rest of the onion and garlic and fry until brown and crisp and place in a cup. Fry the potatoes and the white vermicelli and mix together in a bowl. Place clean bean sprouts in a bowl. Put four large bowls of bouillon on the table and for each bowl add: first the potatoes and white vermicelli, the bean sprouts, the shredded chicken breast, the fried onion and garlic and the shredded Chinese cabbage. Sprinkle chopped cooked egg on top.

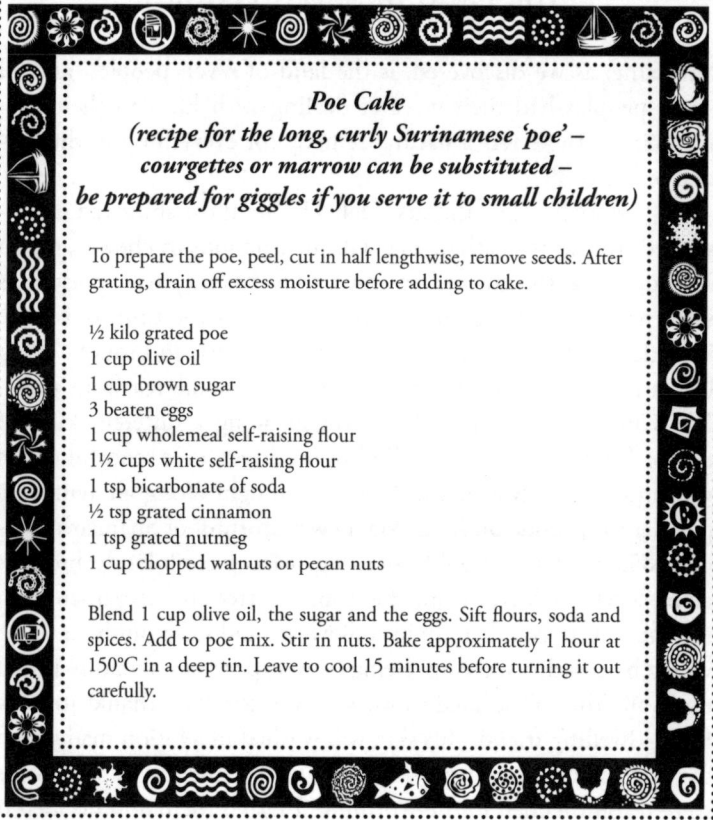

Poe Cake
(recipe for the long, curly Surinamese 'poe' –
courgettes or marrow can be substituted –
be prepared for giggles if you serve it to small children)

To prepare the poe, peel, cut in half lengthwise, remove seeds. After grating, drain off excess moisture before adding to cake.

½ kilo grated poe
1 cup olive oil
1 cup brown sugar
3 beaten eggs
1 cup wholemeal self-raising flour
1½ cups white self-raising flour
1 tsp bicarbonate of soda
½ tsp grated cinnamon
1 tsp grated nutmeg
1 cup chopped walnuts or pecan nuts

Blend 1 cup olive oil, the sugar and the eggs. Sift flours, soda and spices. Add to poe mix. Stir in nuts. Bake approximately 1 hour at 150°C in a deep tin. Leave to cool 15 minutes before turning it out carefully.

2

The Land of Seven Peoples

Suriname, as we discovered, is the land of seven peoples, and all seven peoples had their ways of dealing with life and their own medicines. There was a natural remedy for everything in the garden or the bush.

When we had sore throats, Mabel brought the shiny red moon-shaped fruit of the cashew tree with instructions to chew it, on no account to eat the raw cashew nut attached as they were poisonous until processed. It was juicy and dry at the same time and while it made the throat burn it seemed to help. Sarinah brought along leaves in a plastic bag with instructions to make tea from them. KJ's Chinese PA at the office brought along a different kind of tea for fevers. Shankar, the Hindustani driver, ever scornful of the ministrations of Mabel and Sarinah, brought along an ayurvedic powder to sprinkle on food. Mabel was scornful of Shankar's powder. When KJ had trouble sleeping, Mabel confidently brought along a bag of leaves from the 'soursop' tree in her garden with instructions to put them in his pillowcase and sleep on them. After which he couldn't wake up. Being of an experimental nature I tried them all. They all seemed to work – even for Star. Thanks to rain-forest-dwelling friends, his skin was washed in a lotion made from the 'red cotton' tree (redi katoen) and ground-up papaya seeds were recommended for de-worming. I tasted them and decided it was too high a price to pay. Even for Star.

We were beginning to realise the kindness and humanity of the Surinamese peoples, and the closeness of their bond with nature. We were also beginning to realise the reality of the 'seven cultures'.

Once a week on Saturday mornings, we went for an outing downtown through the main market to buy tropical flowers from the flower sellers outside the Torarica Hotel. In the central market crowds were milling around the car, darting across the road laden with baskets and bags of fruit and vegetables. Every kind of person was there; Indian women in glowing silk saris, tall men with glowing black skins and Dutch features, small bespectacled Chinese gentlemen with wispy beards, and stocky, solid Amerindian folk in bright colours, wearing sandals made of car tyres. The entire history of Suriname was out on the street before us. But what was this history?

How was it that here, on the north coast of South America, so many races had washed up over the centuries? Where had they all come from, and why?

The earliest inhabitants were the ancestors of the present-day Amerindians. Dutch traders came to the 'Wild Coast' followed by English settlers in the mid seventeenth century led by Lord Willoughby, the then governor of Barbados. He annexed thirty thousand hectares and built a fort and named the settlement – predictably – 'Willoughby land'. During the 1650s, during a religious persecution, Jewish settlers from Brazil came to the colony too, attracted by the promise of religious freedom. They lived in the area known as the Jodensavanne (the Jewish Savannah), south of Paramaribo. Traces of the old Jewish settlement still survive, a collection of atmospheric ruins, brooding, silent and overgrown in the steaming tropical forest. In the hot haunting atmosphere birds call and scarlet heliconias flash among the dark green forest growth. The old graveyards are still there, one for the Jewish settlers, one for their slaves. Names are still legible, the human stories forgotten.

In 1667 seven Dutch ships from Zeeland sailed up the Suriname river to the alarm of the settlers. The invasion was led by Abraham Crijnssen who captured Fort Willoughby and renamed it Fort Zeelandia. It still remains on the foreshore in the centre of Paramaribo, an octagonal stone keep, massive and fortified. No longer a bastion of defence, it is now used for national occasions, performances of multicultural dance and art exhibitions. Once a symbol of invasion, it is now a source of national pride and a symbol of unity.

On 31st July 1667, the English and Dutch signed the Treaty of Breda by which the Dutch would occupy Suriname and the British took over a former Dutch colony called New Amsterdam in exchange. New Amsterdam is better known today to most people as New York. With no disrespect to Suriname, the English probably had the best of the bargain.

The English regained Suriname once more, then lost it again to the Dutch in 1668. Finally the Society of Suriname was set up, jointly shared by the city of Amsterdam, the family van Aerssen van Sommelsdijck and the Dutch West India Company. The Company exported goods to Amsterdam – snake wood (a beautiful wood with a sinuous satiny sheen, highly prized by cabinet-makers), coffee, cocoa, and cotton.

With plantations, came slavery. Slave owners in Suriname were renowned for the heights of their opulence and the depths of their cruelty. The life of a slave in Suriname was desperate. The climate was – and is – extreme, the swampy polders harboured mosquitoes and disease, and the heavy clay made work doubly difficult. Word leaked out of monstrous cruelty. One planter's wife, Susanna Duplessis was infamous for her unspeakable sadism. In a fit of jealousy she is reputed to have cut off the breasts of a beautiful slave and served them to her husband for his dinner. But she was not alone. Human beings were starved, mutilated and punished in unimaginably sadistic and brutal ways for trivial offences, and used as human targets for 'sport'. Voltaire, in chapter nineteen of Candide, described a slave met 'at Suriname' who had lost his left leg and his right hand.

Candide asks: 'Was it Mynheer Vanderdendur that used you in this cruel manner?'

'Yes, sir,' said the negro. 'It is the custom here. They give a pair of cotton drawers twice a year, and that is all our covering. When we labour in the sugar-works, and the mill happens to snatch hold of a finger, they instantly chop off our hand and when we attempt to run away, they cut off a leg. Both these cases have happened to me and it is at this expense that you eat sugar in Europe.'

John Gabriel Stedman, a young army officer, came to Suriname in 1772. He was part of an expedition to capture escaped slaves.

But appalled by the cruelty he saw he recorded it in his *Narrative of a Five-Years Expedition against the Revolted Negroes of Surinam*. His tales became well known, and gained further fame by being illustrated by William Blake.

Present-day Suriname is shot through with memories and traditions from the days of slavery. People torn from their families and tribes in West Africa, brought across the ocean in appalling conditions and sold, found themselves flung together in mixed groups from different regions, and different African countries. Uprooted individuals, they lived side by side, shared their living space, their work and their hardships, but they had no common language. Communication was essential for survival. Workers needed to understand what was required of them – quickly – if they were to escape punishment or death. It must have concentrated the mind wonderfully. But slaves in Suriname were forbidden to speak Dutch, which was reserved as the language of the masters. Colonial rules severely limited contacts between the settlers and their slaves. The intermediaries were Creole-speaking foremen. And so a common language began to evolve, a patois composed of elements of English, French, Dutch, Portuguese, and African languages. Originally called 'Taki Taki' (or 'Talk Talk') it is today known as 'Sranaan Tongo' – Surinamese tongue. Created in times of hardship out of necessity it was a language for expressing urgent practicalities. There would have been initially little time or spirit for poetry or playing with words. Other, parallel languages evolved, too; slaves would pass messages in songs, music and imitation bird calls, and female slaves spoke volumes in the ways they tied and arranged their starched headdresses.

A golden opportunity came for the slaves in 1712. The French admiral Jacques Cassard, with thirty-eight vessels, sailed up the Suriname river and laid siege to Paramaribo. At night ships slipped past the city to attack and pillage plantations further up-river. Planters fled. It was a now or never chance. Unsupervised slaves must have been thrilled to help the French plunder the estates before they fled into the jungle. It was unexplored and virtually impenetrable to the settlers. Before this, small numbers of slaves had escaped from time to time, but now this larger group of escapees had stolen arms and began to organise themselves. They attacked isolated plantations, freeing more slaves and stealing more arms, ammunition, farm implements and seed. Hundreds, then thousands of escaped slaves began to build a new society – the Maroons. There are five major Maroon tribes still in existence today: the Djuka, the Saramaccaner, the Matuwari, Paramaccaner, and the Quinti.

Each of these peoples has its own oral history telling of the beginnings of this new society. They refer to these early years as 'Fesitem' (first time) and the Saramaccaners speak of their ancestors such as Lanu and Ayako. The story of their escape, and their subsequent hardships and adventures, helped by friendly Amerindians, is part of Saramaccan folklore.

In 1799 the British came again. Now was the time of Napoleon. The Abolition of Slavery Act was passed in the British Parliament in 1807, making it illegal for any British subject to trade in slaves in any part of the British Commonwealth. This act applied in Suriname while under British rule, but when Suriname was returned to the Dutch in 1816 after the defeat of Napoleon it no longer applied and slavery resumed. It lasted for another forty-seven years, until 1863. Anyone with the misfortune to be a slave in Suriname would not be released until 1873. And as in other Caribbean islands, even after slavery was officially abolished they were obliged to continue working for a pittance for their former masters. To this day, a favourite bracelet worn in Suriname consists of a gold band, snipped, with a gap in the metal. It is high fashion and decorative, and as clearly as the emancipation statue in Paramaribo it commemorates the cutting of slave manacles at emancipation.

After slavery ended plantation owners saw their huge tracts of land in danger of falling into agricultural ruin. They imported workers under 'indentured labour' schemes. Chinese workers were brought from the Netherlands East Indies, Indian labourers from the Indian sub-continent (still known as 'Hindustanis' despite the fact that 'Hindustan' no longer exists) and workers from Java. With the racial groups came their spices and foodstuffs, herbs and plants, as well as their languages, dance and musical instruments. Now when Surinamers return to Africa, India, China, or Java, it is a Rip van Winkle experience. They are no longer at home in the 'homelands' that have figured in the dreams of generations. In a modern world they find that they are speaking the language of their ancestors, cooking as great-great-grandparents cooked and performing dances that are no longer remembered.

In our own close contacts we had a small microcosm of this history. Mabel, whose forebears were both African and Indian, Sarinah and Marmin from Java, Shankar, a Hindustani, Max Chin a Sen, the jeweller and grower of heliconias. Names such as 'Freedman' and 'Freeperson' were touching and common. Every day, every contact was an encounter with the multicoloured memories trailed by Suriname's history.

Since Suriname had always been a multiracial society, the topic of racial inheritance was a source of interest and fascination. At the dinner table one might hear a remark such as: 'Well, I'm one-tenth Chinese and one-quarter Amerindian but what about you – where do you get those Chinese eyes?' And the conversation would go on into genealogy and the ancestors who had landed in Suriname centuries ago. Coming from the apartheid-ridden atmosphere of South Africa, where race was a cause of separation, this openness was refreshing.

Dear Mabel was a fertile source of information about Suriname and all things Surinamese. She coached me in the names of plants, flowers, vegetables and fruit. Every shopping basket that tumbled its jewel-coloured contents on to the kitchen table had a story to tell.

There was a green vegetable that we were learning to love called Tyre Blat. It looked like a decorative pot plant – similar to the southern African 'elephant ears' but cooked like sweet spinach. Bitawiri, bitter weed, was another green vegetable – small leaves that tasted horribly bitter when raw, but cooked into a sweet green mass. Equally surprising was lotus root – lotus flowers, saucer-sized, and a gorgeous hot pink – which perfumed the muddy canals in Indian areas of the town. Despite their sacred connotations they were energetically grubbed up by workers with their clothes hitched up to the waist, and the roots were sold as a delicacy. The flowers scented a room for days, and when dried their bright yellow centres, which looked like tiny watering can nozzles, were much in demand in European countries for 'dried arrangements'. We learned, too, that in Suriname oranges should be called 'greens', since they were bright green balls, only orange on the inside. There was a sneaking belief among Surinamers that the Spanish sprayed their oranges with some kind of bright orange paint at night. In fact, it is the cold temperatures at night in Mediterranean countries that cause the fruit to colour.

Most surprising was the fish. Mabel bargained for an endless variety of them and brought them all home festooned on her bicycle. They were all most wonderfully named in Sranaan Tongo according to their bizarre characteristics. There was 'Queery Man', 'Wet Wettie', 'Bang Bang', 'Banga Basha' (they obviously put up a fight!) plus Dogo Tootie ('dog's tooth') and 'Candra Tiki' (meaning 'candlestick' – a long narrow fish).

Sometimes Mabel's forays to the market were not completely successful. One day I asked her to get some honey and she came back with the information: 'Thee honey it was nowhere to be found, but they will send some come any one day!'

Together with Mabel's delightful brand of English, Sranaan Tongo was an endless source of interest and delight. KJ was the 'Biggie Mannie', hot water was 'Fiah Watra', and 'shut the door!' was 'shuttie doro'! On a rainforest visit KJ swears he heard 'Askie thattie mannie there!' in response to a question.

Areas where the river water ran soft and dark coloured by dissolved rainforest leaf-mould were known as 'Blakawatra'. And there was an area in the centre of Paramaribo called 'Pullapanty' because in the old days youngsters would take off their clothes there to swim across a stream.

One day Mabel called me to the window with great excitement, to look at a small brown bird.

'That is the Gado bird, Mevrouw!' she said. 'We have good luck to have him in the garden!'

When I looked enquiring, she explained. It was the God-bird, a very special bird who cared for the young of other birds when they fell out of the nests.

The next day, looking out of the dining room window, we saw it happening. A young brown and yellow bird was learning to fly on a tree near the window. He hopped from the high branches to those lower down, fluttering his wings with each hop. On the other branches of the tree, and on the ground, a dozen or so small birds were gathered, watching anxiously, prepared to repel any predators who might want to take advantage of the situation. Perhaps Mabel was right.

Birds were a part of life in Suriname. The dawn chorus was deafening and endlessly varied. And on the 'Onafhankelijkheidsplein' (Independence Square) in the centre of town, there is a widely spaced circle of mysterious little stands, each built to hold a birdcage. At sunrise during the weekends, Chinese men bring their cherished birds – usually 'Twa-twas' – to compete for prizes in bird-singing competitions. In most towns people take their dogs for a walk and the birds fly free. In Paramaribo people take their birds for a walk or a bicycle ride, carefully carrying their small cages – and the dogs run free.

After our illness and the quiet Christmas, we left to visit my mother in Australia and to celebrate KJ's birthday there. Circumnavigating the world may have seemed like an unusual route to recuperation but it seemed to work. The Australian birthday party was full of relatives and friends, good food, and a bush band playing Irish tunes.

When we arrived back our Surinamese friends were incensed. This was a 'Bigi Yari!' – a Big Year – a birthday ending in a '0'. There had to be a Surinamese celebration so that they could all celebrate too. I enquired how a 'Bigi Yari' should be done and with the help of friends and office staff we set about planning. The Surinamese birthday celebration required an arch of lights around the gate from Benny's Indian Lighting so everyone would know it was a party. It also had to have a Surinamese musical trio of mellow and benevolent old musicians playing traditional tunes, a dance troupe of Cottomiessies (Cotton Missies) and Moksi Alesi (rice) to eat.

The evening began with a trumpeter at the gate, playing a discordant version of 'When the Saints Go Marching In!' Behind him followed a procession of twelve 'Cottomiessies' – a group of local women who went round to parties dressed in the elaborately frilled and folded cotton dresses and headdresses of slave times. They performed a stately circle dance of staccato walking steps, and explained the various costumes – the house worker, the fruit seller, the flower seller, the fish seller and the lady of the town. In the time of slavery, the slave owners' wives were decidedly not happy for their husbands to see beautiful young black women going around bare-breasted. They gave the female slaves gifts of cloth for Christmas and instructed them to make it into clothes. Since they were given neither instructions nor needles and thread, the slaves cleverly evolved ways of folding and starching the cloths, which they wore in layers approximating to the fashionably draped clothes of their mistresses. And above the clothes were the elaborately folded headdresses, each one conveying a message about the status or availability of the wearer. Folded one way a headdress might mean 'I am not interested in men!' and folded another way and it would be: 'Meet me at the corner!'

The dance finished, the Cottomiessies began to walk in a circle to the music, inviting gentlemen from the party to remove one layer of cloth each time the music stopped. It was a sort of musical striptease. The prettiest and youngest girl was chosen for this exercise. There were sixteen layers of cloth to remove, leaving her attired from neck to knee in long frilly underwear. The benevolent Catholic bishop, Bishop Zichem, was the last man to be chosen and he gently removed the rose from between her teeth.

In normal times, life continued much as it did during the first year. We were not exactly resigned to the endless sticky heat but as the thermostat showed no sign of turning down, we turned up air conditioners and fans, and sat outside when we could. Houses with a second storey and balcony, or those near the river, might be cooled by an evening breeze, but we were inland in a single-storey house enclosed by high walls. Even so, the night guards wore knitted balaclavas when the temperature fell to anything below 27°C.

Sometimes it rained, often in the early evening. The perfume of hot dry earth would rise into the air as the rain began. Coolness would settle on to the evening. And after the rain as we went out to breathe the freshness of it all, tiny tree frogs would start up their chirping in the trees, as hundreds of glow-worms illuminated the branches, turning their tail lights on-off on-off like minuscule flying Christmas lights.

During the day we shared the garden not only with tropical flowers and songbirds but with something else. Every day large purple droppings appeared on the garden paths. What could it be? I fantasised about monkeys, fruit-eating bats – even giant squirrels. But the culprits were very large, fluorescent green iguanas, mini-dragons which could be anything from two to four feet long, with fearsome spikes down their backs. The first time I saw one, I sent KJ out with a broom to chase it away, for fear that Star might tangle with it (and to be honest, I didn't much relish the idea of tangling with it myself). Fortunately, as far as we know, there was no dog-iguana confrontation although Star was on sniffing acquaintance with their purple droppings and with their smaller emerald and electric-blue relatives. He peaceably enjoyed the iguanas, and the birds and all of the small events of the house and garden, but his big excitement was the weekly trip to town.

He was the only English bull terrier in Suriname, quite possibly the only one who had ever been seen there, and when he travelled by car he caused so much stir that we might have had a lion or a leopard on board. KJ drove and Star sat with me in the back in the little Japanese car. He was balanced on a little wooden bench that KJ had specially made so that he could put his head out of the window. We had not expected such instant celebrity. Bull terriers have massive heads and chests, and people probably concluded that the rest of the dog was to scale. Certainly an English bull terrier in a car on a Saturday morning in Suriname's central market was an event.

Star leant out the window grinning and panting at everything he saw. The effect on the colourful crowd at the market was electric. Cyclists wobbled and fell off their bikes when his grinning teeth passed close by, buses from the country screeched to a halt and tilted to one side as the occupants dashed across the aisle to get a better look, parents held up small children to see him. Indian ladies in silk saris shrieked in terror and pulled each other back, little ragged urchins ran behind the car barking and shouting 'Doggie doggie!' and 'Pit bull!' – carloads of children fell about laughing, and the young news vendor near the Presidential Palace kept his distance and was strangely unwilling to make a sale. A well-dressed Chinese lady driving a long black Mercedes stopped next to us at a traffic light, wound down the window, crossed her eyes, stuck out her tongue and panted back at him in imitation. Star enjoyed it all. So did we. It was like travelling with Marilyn Monroe in the back seat of the car.

Star was tranquilly accepted by the kind household staff. They patiently opened and closed doors for him to let him in and out. If it was raining outside the front door he would look disconsolate and come back in. He would then ask to be let out the back door just in case it might not be raining there as well. He would bark once to be let back in and wait politely. Then he would bark twice. If still no door opener was forthcoming he would utter a salvo of a dozen or so woofs, and keep it up until someone came. Sarinah loved to brush him and would give him surreptitious hugs when she thought no one was looking. Mabel kept an eye on his well-being. I was taken aback early in our stay by a loud and cheerful morning greeting from her, saying: 'Morning Mevrouw, Star, he pooped good this morning!'

One Saturday morning, Sarinah was hanging out some washing on the line. KJ and I were inspecting the garden beds where plants were burgeoning after the rain. We noticed a new, strong creeper springing up. Knowing that most Javanese people loved plants and were talented gardeners, KJ turned to Sarinah and asked in Nederlands: 'What's this plant, Sarinah?'

Sarinah looked over dismissively from her washing line, and said briefly: 'Vogelpoep Mijnheer!' ('Bird poo, sir!')

Having expected some poetic name for the plant, we were thrown into a fit of the giggles, and repaired hastily to the laundry room to stuff handkerchiefs in our mouths.

Sarinah, as mentioned before, operated best in tandem with Mabel. Mabel did the communicating, organised the tasks and gave the orders. Gentle little Sarinah was happiest following instructions. When Mabel had her annual holidays, Sarinah was less than half herself. She crept around the house in uncanny silence, sweeping, and polishing, she cooked the lunch in a silent kitchen, and it was obvious she missed her 'sergeant major'. On one occasion, for some reason, I was away for part of this time and poor Sarinah, a good Muslim wife, was *alone* in the house with KJ. Coming down the passage in the eerie silence, they accidentally met at a corner. With an 'aaiieeee!' Sarinah leapt three feet in the air and vanished panic-stricken towards the kitchen.

In one of these Mabel-less periods, KJ and I were sitting in the dining room, at the end of lunch, fending off mosquitoes in a desultory sort of way, when Sarinah came in. She had served the food, but she had obviously rehearsed something to say in Nederlands. She drew her very small frame up as tall as it would go and announced, 'Mijnheer, Mevrouw, I have upset the cat's bum.' And then she disappeared.

We looked at each other. What was that we had just heard? We didn't have a cat. And if we did, how could that particular portion of its anatomy be upset? All kinds of mad images raced through our minds, of upended cats with offended expressions on their faces. Trying to be sensible, and not give way totally to hysterical laughter, we thought of possible alternatives. Was it something to do with a 'baum' – a tree, perhaps – but what tree? And how could that be upset either?

Finally, after twenty minutes or so of mad laughter, the sort you just can't stop, KJ spluttering, and with tears streaming down his face, gasped: 'I've got it! Sarinah has replaced the gas canister for the kitchen stove.'

'Ik heb opgezet de gasbom!' ('I have set up the gas bomb!')

Dear little Sarinah, having struggled manfully, had replaced the huge, heavy gas canister behind the gas stove and reconnected it. And she came to tell us about it. Thank heavens we contained our laughter until after she had left the room.

There were other characters in the Suriname play. Marmin, the Javanese gardener, was a tall, shadowy man, who gently tended his plants wearing a floppy cloth hat. He materialised and dematerialised from tree to tree and spoke nothing but Javanese, so that all communication had to be done with energetic digging and clipping motions. Marmin was a sensitive soul and the plants loved him and grew apace. In any case, in Suriname, the hardest task was to *stop* plants from growing. If a house was left for a month, it disappeared under vegetation and had to be dug out.

There were three office drivers. Shankar, the senior driver, was a handsome and dapper Hindustani gentleman, with a small Mephistophelian beard and a strut. He taught us a lot about the local Hindustani world view; namely, if there was the slightest chance to do business in life, it would be foolish not to profit by it. It was a variation on the Portuguese philosophy of 'esquemas' (schemes), which we had learnt in Angola. Together with 'my rittel brudder' Shankar was frequently involved in deals that this time, for sure, would make his fortune. They never did and like a local 'Dell Boy' he was chronically short of money as a result and needed pay-day loans. He liked driving the big official car, which could sometimes be seen in unlikely corners of Paramaribo, as he took in a visit to a business contact en route to the office. He hated being caught out in anything, and if any scratches appeared on the white car, they would be magicked away by a judicious application of Tipp-Ex 'borrowed' from the office, in the fond belief that KJ would never notice.

Driver number two was also Hindustani. He was young, smiling, handsome and charming, and an aficionado of bodybuilding which added to his film star looks. Unfortunately his nemesis came when it was discovered that he was moonlighting on a second job in duty hours. Good try, Akash! I missed his charm.

Driver number three was Michel. Michel was a seven-foot tall Dutchman in every respect, with features straight out of a Breughel painting. The interesting anomaly was that he had African ancestry and his very Dutch features were painted in the beautiful shades of a blue-black skin. He was the most obliging soul, like an affable

Great Dane puppy with enormous feet. He was always willing to drive the forty-five kilometres to the airport after hours to rescue a late diplomatic bag, or to put up balloons for Europe Day. He it was who rescued branches of the old mahogany trees being cut down in 'de Mahonielaan' (Mahogany Street) and brought them to the house with gangling diffidence so that KJ could use the wood in his workshop to make jewellery boxes.

With all of this cultural intermingling, we found ourselves invited to wildly contrasting events. When driver Shankar's 'little brother' was married we were invited to the wedding, which took place in traditional style over three days. On this evening the bridegroom's ceremonies had taken place, and the guests were invited to Shankar's new, almost-completed house for a feast. We picked our way across a yard still strewn with building stones and concrete and joined the wedding party on a long veranda area. It was crowded with people dressed in their wedding best. Saris shone and gold jewellery glowed underneath the light. There was a crisis in the kitchen. A dozen ladies were chattering in high-pitched voices and menfolk were sent running in all directions. The water in the kitchen had cut off and a large plastic rain barrel had to be manhandled in with maximum drama, and placed in position so the festival could continue.

The food was served, roti and curry, with plastic tubs of rice, salad and an assortment of spices, chutneys and condiments. Long tables were laid out down each side of the veranda. Men were seated along one wall, women along the other. The older members of the family were served first, with impressive respect and care. The proud servers were the women who had done the cooking, moving gracefully and accepting due thanks. Younger generations waited patiently, talking among themselves, on chairs and benches at the other end of the space. Their turn would come.

After the meal the dancing began. Indian music with a beat was playing on the tape deck. With respect and courtliness Shankar invited me to dance. Wondering how to play this, I glanced around, but there was no help. I mimicked what he was doing and hoped it was acceptable. And so with our hands raised above our heads, we gyrated with swinging hips to the beat, Shankar and I, turning and twisting in circles, round and round each other. The sound of the music rang out in the steamy night drowning the sound of the cicadas.

As well as the 'Hindustanis' from the Indian sub-continent, Amerindians still lived in the Surinamese forest. My first rainforest experience took place at Redi Doti (Red Dirt), forty-five kilometres south of Paramaribo, near the Jodensavanne. KJ had visited the area. He noticed massive trees felled by international logging companies, left discarded in the forest, due to some imperfection. There were millions of trees to choose from, was the philosophy. Why bother about wasting a few!

Turning to the leader of the Amerindian community he asked: 'Could those be used?'

A torrent of explanation followed – yes they could but they were too big to transport to a sawmill for processing.

'Could you manage to get them to the village?' Again the answer, after much discussion, was 'Yes!' A small portable sawmill would be needed to turn the giant logs into planks. And so a project was born.

The day of the project opening arrived. The journey to Redi Doti was over roads already ploughed up by massive logging trucks which now well merited the name 'Red Dirt'. In places the truck ruts were so deep it was hard to know where to drive. The forest on either side of the road was studded with giant traveller's palms and banana-like trees as big as oaks. It was a dense impenetrable wall. Easy to imagine walking in there and never finding a way out. Stand still for a while in the forest and you will be overgrown by lianes, we had heard.

The little forest community of Redi Doti was agog with excitement. A small sawmill had been purchased, reconditioned and was ready for action. It was lying in a forest clearing, endearingly decorated with intricately woven palm leaves, and studded with red and yellow forest flowers. The brand new timber dais where the speeches would be made was decorated with palm leaves and flowers, too, as was the newly built shelter where the bar was set up and a small local band was playing. All of the visitors were given a posy as they arrived.

Speeches of thanks were made. KJ and I, representing the donor agency for this sawmill, were ceremonially draped with shawls. They would once have been cloaks of woven birds' feathers. They were still beautiful, but now they were made of crochet wool, the coloured threads interwoven like plumes. They were regal and beautiful – and they were very hot! The wife of the headman grabbed me with a firm claw-like hand and took pains to impress me that this shawl was only on loan and must be given back. We were taken on a tour, walking up and down the wooden houses set in neat rows, inspecting the new buildings and the objects that had already been made using the new equipment.

And then the new machine was started up. Still in its party dress of woven palms and flowers the sturdy iron machine gave a roar, emitted a few puffs of smoke, and set to work chewing up a log, chips flying. Serenaded by the local band, we sat on benches underneath a flowery wooden and pine branch canopy, and listened to plans for all the things that were going to be built in the future with this amazing gift. Without quite knowing how it happened, I found that I had committed the Diplomatic Ladies' Association to the presentation of new sewing machines for a community hall that had yet to be built. Never had a small, unpretentious piece of equipment brought so much excitement and happiness. It looked as though one simple small sawmill would be the magic tool to transform the lives of the entire community.

Later in the year there was the grand opening of a clinic at Stoelmanseiland (Stoelmann's Island), in the rainforest. We were invited to attend. The only way in was by plane and canoe. Dressed in best rainforest gear and sensible shoes we set off. The flight would leave from the tiny Zorg en Hoop (Care and Hope) airport near the house. A variety of invited guests were waiting there. One tall gentleman, the proprietor of Paramaribo's only health shop, was brandishing a bottle of echinacea extract, and proclaiming that he never got malaria, because he always took this whenever he went into the forest. The smallest of small planes came, and we were whisked up and out beyond Paramaribo, over the rainforest – a green sea of broccoli heads, soft and bubbly, interspersed with occasional bright yellow foliage where a huge 'greenheart' tree had been growing for centuries, undisturbed by exploiting loggers. We landed in a steamy outpost manned by Medecins Sans Frontières. A short explanation of their work in a tiny, open-sided clinic and we were led to the bank of the river where long, motorised dug-out canoes were waiting, each one manned by a strong bare-chested Maroon boatman. We set off down the river. Rainforest lined the banks. There were few birds; nothing broke the silence except the sound of the boats. The river was a series of rapids. At each level the navigators jumped into the water to push and shove the canoes over and between the rocks. While the pushing and scraping was happening, we sat upright feeling useless, not knowing what else to do, like po-faced early explorers. We only lacked the pith helmets.

The boats came to ground on Stoelmann's Island, and we were pulled in to the shallows like Captain Cook landing on Tahiti. Greeted not by hostile islanders, but by TV cameras, we were helped out and on to dry land hoping not to fall flat on our faces in front of the Suriname Evening News. An assortment of dignitaries was waiting, and the new, small clinic was opened with speeches and ceremony. Coca-Cola was served with curling sandwiches and dry biscuits.

Then the local Maroon community danced to show their pleasure at the new clinic. It was the girls who danced – the young men drummed on heavy hollow logs. The girls were young – in their teens, with shiny dark skins and tightly curling hair. In their ears and around their necks they wore an astonishing amount of glittering pure gold jewellery, roughly made in chunky chains and spirals. It was gold panned from the rivers by the community, and beaten by local craftsmen into symbols of the owner's standing and wealth. On the top half of their bodies they wore Western bras (in generous sizes) and their lower halves were wrapped in short, brightly coloured cloths, roughly hand-embroidered with geometric patterns. And how they danced! As the drums beat, they bent forward at right angles from the waist, buttocks jutting, and deeply bending their knees, they pulsated and vibrated their whole bodies as their heels jarred rapidly up and down on the earth. It was driving, sensuous, primal and orgasmic.

And then there were the Javanese Kuda Lumping dancers. We had been invited by the German consul and his wife, a cultured and artistic Surinamese couple, to a day on their historic coffee plantation across the river from Paramaribo. We waited on the waterfront for the boat that would transport us back into the seventeenth century. This was one of the plantations from which the planters and slaves had run when the French sailed up the Suriname river. The seventeenth-century house was wooden, cool and dark. We saw coffee production as it was still done in Suriname, by hand, the beans husked in iron drums and then spread out on the ground to dry, as it had been for hundreds of years.

After lunch a special treat was promised. But it was hot. Very hot. First we were led down a flight of wooden stairs to the area underneath the house, among the tall wooden stilt foundations. A dozen or more coloured and fringed hammocks or 'Hangmatten' swung invitingly, and a series of cane lounges and chairs beckoned. The guests were invited to rest. We took our ease, like the planters of old. Our eyes became heavy in the heat, and the conviviality segued seamlessly into a shared diplomatic and consular afternoon nap.

A team of Javanese men approached. They made themselves ready for the performance. It was introduced as a 'special kind of dance'. The members of a gamelan orchestra brought their horizontal hanging bells, sat down on the ground and began to play. Men entered carrying roughly carved wooden horses. With these they pranced and danced, egged on by the leader of the group who seemed to be controlling them with a strange hypnotic power. As the music speeded up and the dance progressed the trance dancers metamorphosed into horses. They whinnied and neighed, they trotted and galloped and reared, they tossed their manes and mated. Sometimes they fell on the ground, foaming and were raised up by the leader. They ate bundles of grass and hay and drank from buckets. With superhuman strength, the small wiry men broke tree branches and bent iron bars.

Some dancers began to change into other animals. Monkey-like they nimbly scampered up the trees. They sat there, scratching and chattering and eyeing the spectators as though planning mischief. They were thrown bananas and threw back the skins. A chicken was caught and was rescued from imminent decapitation. Some became dogs and, barking, scampered on all fours through the bush. Occasionally one would run out of steam and fall to the ground, to be resuscitated by the leader with a sniff of some mysterious substance. The pace of the performance became faster and more frenetic. Part of the audience was fascinated, part frightened, part repelled. We felt we were in the midst of some ancient rite when the barriers between man and nature had loosened. There was a strange energy in the air, a sense of barely controlled wildness. There was no recognisable choreography – the performance or ritual took on its own momentum. When the frenzied energy was spent, it died down of its own accord, the gamelan playing faded, and the players departed.

All of these cultures, Amerindian, African, East Indian, and Javanese had lived together in this rainforest environment for centuries. They had existed in harmony, each following its own way, while accepting the rest. Children grew up knowing there were many ways to live, many ways to think, and many ways to dance. There was no need for classes in 'multiculturalism' in Suriname. It was reality.

One evening at Fort Zeelandia, that massive old symbol of conquest and repression, the multicultural Suriname that had been created over the centuries staged a concert. It was as though characters from centuries past stepped out of history to dance and sing together. Groups of exquisite Indian classical dancers from the Indian Cultural Centre evoked Hindu deities with classical poses and hand gestures, tiny Javanese girls floated across the stage with flowers in their hair, recreating temple dance with fragile, breakable limbs, and solid Maroon dancers throbbed, gyrated and stamped to the beat of drums. There were Maroon drummers playing drums hewn out of tree trunks, Indian tassa drummers, sitar players and a gamelan orchestra.

And then at the end of the evening, the dancers switched. The Indian dancers bent from the waist and began stamping their feet, with extraordinary elegance, the Maroon troupe tried their best to do the subtle hand gestures of temple dancing, tiny Javanese ladies became Indian. Each group having confirmed its own tradition, it was a demonstration of openness to each other's cultures, and perhaps a glimpse into a seamless universal future when differences might be both celebrated and transcended.

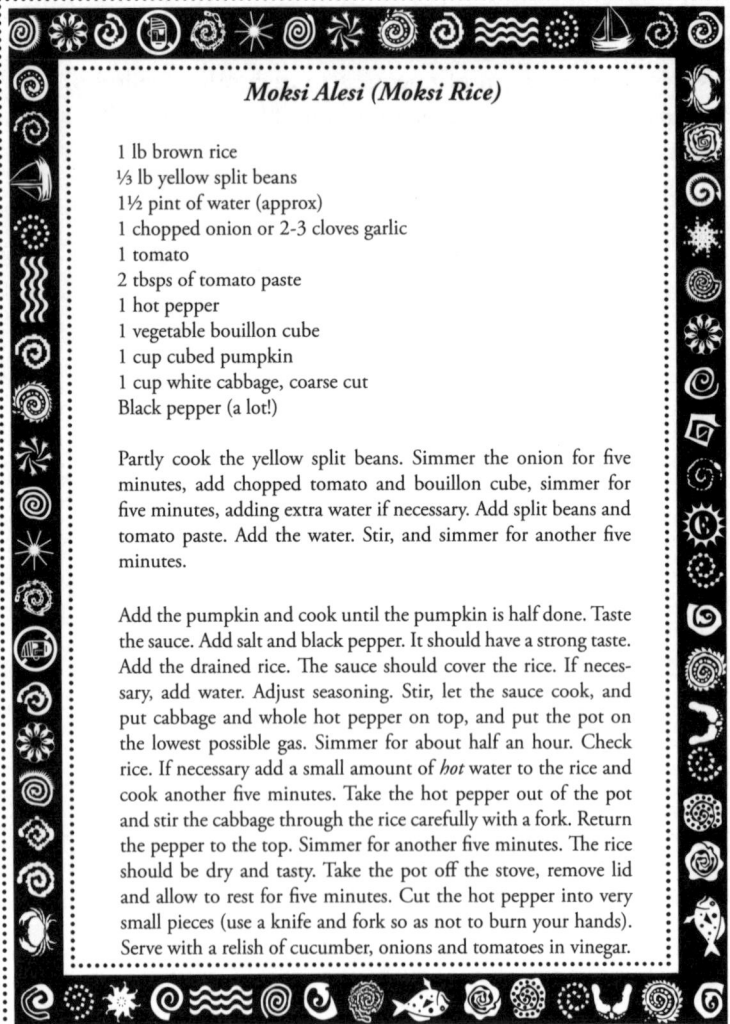

Moksi Alesi (Moksi Rice)

1 lb brown rice
⅓ lb yellow split beans
1½ pint of water (approx)
1 chopped onion or 2-3 cloves garlic
1 tomato
2 tbsps of tomato paste
1 hot pepper
1 vegetable bouillon cube
1 cup cubed pumpkin
1 cup white cabbage, coarse cut
Black pepper (a lot!)

Partly cook the yellow split beans. Simmer the onion for five minutes, add chopped tomato and bouillon cube, simmer for five minutes, adding extra water if necessary. Add split beans and tomato paste. Add the water. Stir, and simmer for another five minutes.

Add the pumpkin and cook until the pumpkin is half done. Taste the sauce. Add salt and black pepper. It should have a strong taste. Add the drained rice. The sauce should cover the rice. If necessary, add water. Adjust seasoning. Stir, let the sauce cook, and put cabbage and whole hot pepper on top, and put the pot on the lowest possible gas. Simmer for about half an hour. Check rice. If necessary add a small amount of *hot* water to the rice and cook another five minutes. Take the hot pepper out of the pot and stir the cabbage through the rice carefully with a fork. Return the pepper to the top. Simmer for another five minutes. The rice should be dry and tasty. Take the pot off the stove, remove lid and allow to rest for five minutes. Cut the hot pepper into very small pieces (use a knife and fork so as not to burn your hands). Serve with a relish of cucumber, onions and tomatoes in vinegar.

3

Travels in Suriname – and Other Places

When we came to Suriname, we thought we were coming to the Caribbean – or was it South America? But somehow in Suriname, with all its variety and fascination, it was hard to know exactly where we were. There was no feeling of Caribbean sea, sand and sun, and no laid-back calypso singers, plenty of palm trees but no steel pan bands. It was on the South American continent but Spanish was not spoken. I was not exactly feeling cheated of Caribbean ambience, but KJ had to go to Antigua for a conference of Caribbean countries, and wives were invited too – so, who would refuse?

We arrived at the Johannes Pengel airport at 8 a.m. for a 10 a.m. plane to Antigua. The airport was suspiciously quiet. There were no passengers. There was no plane. The schedule had changed and the flight had left two hours ago. The airline staff gave us three options: we could fly all the way to Paris and then back to Antigua; we could fly to Miami and then back to Antigua; or we could fly to Cayenne, and connect to Sint Maarten where we would just miss a connection to Antigua. The problem with all these options, apart from the astronomical cost, was that we would miss the conference entirely. Or, since it was an important conference, we could go back to Paramaribo, hire a light plane and fly the relatively short distance to Georgetown, Guyana, where there would be a flight to Antigua in a few hours.

There was just time to speed back to the office and have the small plane OK'd. KJ threw a few firecrackers at his secretary who had not read the change of timetable properly and we drove around the corner to Zorg en Hoop Airport where there was a three-seater Cessna waiting. Also waiting was a very big Surinamer in military uniform, with large amounts of gold braid on his shoulders – one of the president's aides. To our great surprise he was expecting us.

News travels fast in Paramaribo. It is a small town with a complex network of relationships and favours. In the half hour since we missed the flight the president's aide had heard that we would be taking a small plane to Georgetown. He must have known before we did. Could he come with us? It was urgent. He would pay his share.

'Why not?' said KJ.

The three of us climbed aboard the little plane, and took off over an immensity of green treetops. There was an occasional clearing studded with the thatched huts of an Amerindian village, and an occasional winding river. Nothing else for two hundred miles. We only discovered much later that we were not covered by KJ's insurance from HQ for flying in a single-engine Cessna over vast tracts of rainforest – or anywhere else.

In Georgetown we said goodbye to our large and affable friend. We learned that having exceeded all speed limits to arrive for the 4.15 flight, it was now delayed until 6.15 – a five-hour wait. In any airport this would be boring. In Georgetown Guyana it promised to be excruciating. There were a few plastic chairs in a 'viewing gallery' but it was closed. The entrance to the departures area was deserted, except for the ghost of curries past. The executive lounge was locked. Was it to be five hours standing in the airport?

We were directed through the rain to another area of lounges. A plump and pleasant young woman presided there, wearing the airport uniform of white shirt, black skirt, black shoes and black bobby socks. She sent us up a steep staircase to a door marked VIP. The TV was blaring inside but the door was locked. We all knocked. Nothing. She disappeared to find 'de person wit de key'.

We waited, sweltering, outside two very splendid bathrooms. The toilets and basins were clothed in long skirts of bright pink towelling – with fringes and bobbles. There was neither water nor toilet paper but the general effect was very fine.

An elderly lady's head came bobbing up the stairs. 'Come in, come in,' she said, followed by: 'De door is locked. Who lock dis door?' And she disappeared.

After another hour perching on ledges and standing on one foot after the other, we were let into a huge, splendid and disordered lounge. It had chairs and air conditioning. It also had half a dozen ladies with mops and buckets, who sang lustily as they worked. Then came the ice-breakers and the cup-rattlers. We learned by judicious eavesdropping that President Jagan of Guyana had been there last night and had collapsed in that very lounge with a heart attack. No wonder it was so disarrayed.

We were called over to the BWIA (known locally as Beewee) airline desk and offered a meal voucher for $10 by a kindly young woman.

'Y'all can spend it upstairs in the gallery, but it's closed right now,' she said, 'or you can spend it over there' – gesturing vaguely to something across a car park – 'only its rainin' right now out there. But you spend it somewhere now, mind.'

She was right about the rain.

We managed to spend our voucher on two small tins of peanuts, a dubious-looking hamburger and a bright pink drink. We hurried back to the lounge before anyone could lock it again. Finally, after five hours we took of for Antigua – only to find ourselves grounded for another two hours in Trinidad, Port of Spain. It was a pleasant, brightly painted airport, full of endless souvenirs all made in the shape of steel pans, and populated by immensely tall, handsome, well-built people dressed in colourful, stylish clothes, who sashayed along as if about to break into a dance. Most of them had such panache and verve that the floor shook as they passed.

At midnight we reached Antigua. It looked much the same as anywhere else does at that hour after sixteen hours of travelling.

The next day the island showed its colours. They were blue and white, aquamarine, sea green, gold, and a rainbow of pastels. It had dry, warm air and sea breezes. The sea was turquoise and the houses were painted in pastel colours. It was a watercolour of fishing boats and yachts, and long-legged Rastas riding short-legged donkeys on the mountain roads.

The hotel was created from the ruins of one of the many sugar mills. Only the tower was left and some old copper vats. Antigua had a rich history as a sugar producer, and was reputed to have been one of the Caribbean islands where selective 'slave-breeding' was practised. Tall strong male slaves were used as studs. The early planters wanted to produce strong slaves in the same way that wealthy people today want to produce fast racehorses.

Even while remembering the past, we drank in the beauty of the island. The mornings were windy, and black pelicans rode the currents of air like black kites without a string, swooping down occasionally for a large fish. The markets were full of brightly primitive paintings, in psychedelic colours. At the end of the main street, with its tiny pink and blue and yellow wooden houses, vast cruise liners were moored, towering over the tiny coloured cabins. They appeared silently each morning as if someone had secretly built a skyscraper in the night. We visited Nelson's dockyard, and imagined his fleet moored in the picturesque bay below us, and his romances with local ladies.

A Rasta loomed out of the bushes, picked a leaf of a handy aloe vera plant and offered to sell it to us: 'In case de sun catch yeh nose bad!'

At night in a restaurant there was 'dolphin' on the menu. I froze in dismay until I learned that it was a long, narrow local fish and not a porpoise. And in the same restaurant, we struck up a conversation with a cheerful weather-beaten couple – two ancient mariners in their eighties who had sold their house and intended to sail the seas of the world like reincarnated Flying Dutchmen, if not forever, at least as long as they possibly could.

We returned to Paramaribo in time to welcome a large Mission team from HQ. They had come for meetings with government to plan the next three years of developmental projects. There were ten hectic days of dinners, cocktails, discussions and project excursions. There were exciting plans for a new road west from Paramaribo through the bush and forest, to the town of Niew Nickerie, and one east to Albina, thus linking Suriname with Guyana on the one hand and French Guiana on the other. There was a new ferry to be visited on the borders of Guyana and there were projects in rice and bananas and tourism.

For my part there were 6 a.m. breakfasts to provide before departure, coffee flasks to fill, and muffins to bake for the long road excursions. One morning I was in the kitchen at 3 a.m. kneading bread for fresh bread rolls to be taken on a rainforest excursion. I briefly wondered whether this was really what life should be all about. No doubt the members of the Planning Team just thought the house elves had been at work early, if they gave their picnic a thought at all. I suppose in a sense they were right. I was the house elf.

The ten days over, after one last lunch for everyone, the cars swung out through the gate to take the visitors to the airport. I breathed a sigh of relief, kicked off my shoes, and wandered through the blissfully quiet and empty house. I was looking forward to playing with Star, perhaps reading a book, or catching up with emails. Above all not having to *plan* anything for a few days at least.

After what seemed like no time at all, the phone rang. It was KJ. He was phoning from the airport to say that the visitors' plane had been delayed until 2.30 the following morning. He was bringing them all back again together with the Australian ambassador and his wife from Barbados, and a stray UN representative who was stranded as well.

I opened the fridge and peered inside. It was bare. I looked in the cupboards. We were well and truly eaten out of house and home after the last ten days. There was a bowl of mushroom sauce left over from last night's dinner, some cream, a bit of salad and some fruit. If I had been qualified to multiply loaves and fishes it would have been enough, but I wasn't. Not yet anyway. In the hour's grace as they drove in from the airport I phoned around. The friendly wife of the World Health Organisation representative thought she had a monstrous packet of angel hair pasta in her freezer. I'd never heard of angel hair pasta but anything was worth a try. I leapt into my little car, dashed to her house and 'borrowed' it.

The group arrived. The whole Planning Team plus three, all supremely grateful to be spared a night in the airport. There was an air of relief, fun and hilarity. The Australian ambassador from Barbados was a down-to-earth Aussie who commandeered the drinks cupboard saying: 'At least I can buttle!'

His friendly wife helped mutter incantations in the kitchen so that the mushroom sauce was miraculously expanded. The angel hair pasta was combed into submission with forks when it threatened to stick. We made salad and a huge fruit salad and ate it all on the veranda in the company of night frogs and crickets. It was a hilarious evening, full of the laughter born of thankfulness at being spared a night on concrete airport benches. It ended in KJ's study, watching a video of the newly discovered Riverdance Irish Dance Company. Arms clutched tightly to their virtuous sides, the Irish dancers bounced and twinkled their feet as the VIPs and the Planning Mission slowly subsided into snores on their various chairs and couches. They left at midnight. I took off my shoes and collapsed for the second time in one day.

Ten days later it was St Patrick's Day again. This time we decided to favour Paramaribo with an Irish-flavoured evening. There was some explanation to be done as to who or what St Patrick was, but people seemed interested. I made multiple loaves of Irish soda bread and piled them up in baskets. Margriet, from the Keurslager catering firm, came excitedly with a recipe for Irish stew cut from a Dutch magazine. It seemed to have dumplings that I didn't quite recognise, but otherwise looked like a good stew. We would do Irish cabbage and bacon, and potatoes in their jackets, and gain a wholly undeserved reputation for originality. We put up the regulation arch of lights from Benny's Lighting over the gate (as green as possible) and had lights in the trees. We borrowed a screen so that the Riverdance video could be played again as a salute to Irish culture. We instructed everyone to wear something green but avoided any temptation to serve un-Irish green beer or green rice. We arranged for some Scottish dancing. And thereby hangs a tale.

For several months we had been attending Scottish dancing classes in Paramaribo, mad as that may sound. In this steaming hot Amazonian enclave, we and sixteen Dutch 'Caledonians' would meet once a week to tackled the intricacies of 'Strip the Willow', 'The Scots Bonnet', and 'Miss Mac Bride's Strathspey'. Why?

The Dutch ambassador's daughter was due to marry a Scotsman in Edinburgh at Christmas. The ambassador, a far-sighted fellow, could see the prospect of jigs and reels looming and he didn't want to make a fool of himself. Since the Dutch ambassador was the most important diplomat in Paramaribo, the Dutch community rallied round and found among their number Jobs, a delightful lady who had been part of a championship Scottish dance team in, of all places, Sri Lanka. That's expatriate life for you.

For some reason we thought it would be fun. In theory it was. Once a week, on someone's veranda, we made up sets and practised. Red-faced and sweating, with steam rising from our backs, we danced, perfecting our Dutch numbers as we rhythmically counted steps: *één, twee, drie, vier, vijf, zes, zeven, acht*. We periodically cannoned into the Dutch, always in figure of eight manoeuvres. Collisions only seemed to happen to us. The mystery was solved when we realised, after many weeks, that it was a case of cultural conflict. We write our figure eights from the top, going to the left and down, the Dutch starting from the bottom, going right and up. No wonder there were cross-cultural crashes.

By the time of the St Patrick's party we were rather good (at least we thought so) and were ready to perform in public. So with the justification that 'it's all Celtic anyway', the entire dance team came to the party to give a demonstration of 'Strip the Willow' and each of us kidnapping an astonished guest, we taught them to dance 'The Dashing White Sergeant'.

It was a resounding success. Mabel and Sarinah peeped round the door when the songs and dancing were going on. Mabel pronounced on the lightness of foot of each dancer and enjoyed it greatly when one unfortunate ambassadorial lady dancing in stiletto heels landed on her backside. The very formal French ambassador who normally did a fine line in shoulder-shrugs, observed it all with a Gallic eye and pronounced it approvingly –'Très originale!' – and I surprised my friend Solange, the pretty and lively wife of the Venezuelan ambassador, creeping back to the buffet for her sixth piece of Irish brown bread.

All of these events were hard work, and fun, but they served a serious purpose, in integrating the international community with Surinamers. We, the expatriates, were there, not as ourselves, but as representatives of our countries and organisations and there was work to be done. And work always goes better when relationships are warm and positive. That was my job. Openness and friendliness were attributes highly valued by Surinamers, together with a sense that their country was taken seriously. After hundreds of years of slavery it was as if sensitivity was bred into the DNA. The words 'offence' and 'offensive' were often used – they are words hardly ever heard among English speakers. No one likes to be blamed or made wrong, but it seemed that in Suriname, there was an extreme sensitivity to criticism. Small wonder, when for generations, ancestors had been treated by Europeans as an inferior species. In the house I quickly learned not to find fault. If confronted or challenged, Mabel and Sarinah would freeze and a blind would come down between us. Changes would only take place if, with great respect, I first praised what had been done, and then suggested: 'Next time we could try it this way.'

It was a principle that applied in contacts at all levels. Perhaps it is a good principle in dealing with human beings in general.

From time to time KJ needed to see what was happening on the various projects. The east-west road seemed to be moving very slowly. We planned a trip to French Guiana, one long weekend. We would drive to Albina, along the new road, to check on its progress, then go to Cayenne, to visit the European Space Station at Kourou, and the ironically named Iles du Salut – 'the Island of Health', better known to most English speakers as 'Devil's Island', the notorious prison island made famous by the Dreyfus case, and described in the book *Papillon*.

Once out of Paramaribo, driving east towards Albina, the road was long and dusty. We drove through an area largely inhabited by Javanese families. It had a distinctly South East Asian feel. All the houses had flowers and vegetable gardens. Water buffaloes, dogs and pigs looked fat and well fed. Then the road wound through bush, thickly forested, with here and there, gigantic bananas or Travellers' Palms rearing their heads. From time to time there was a small dusty settlement with ever-drowsier children and thinner dogs draped around the small cabins. As we continued, the state of the road became worse. It was rutted and potholed. Sometimes it disappeared altogether into enormous craters and was shakily re-routed through the bush on a rutted track.

Along the route an assortment of road-working vehicles were parked. For the size of the road project they seemed very small and very sparse. There were no workers to be seen. A suspicion began to dawn in KJ's mind. The recent Planning Mission had inspected the other half of the road en route to Niew Nickerie. The road west from Paramaribo had been thick with road-working vehicles and diligent workers. Could it be perhaps that the contractor had conducted a little stage-setting exercise and positioned most of his equipment there for best effect? And if he didn't have enough equipment for all of his contracts, was he planning to spend all of his time endlessly transferring his trucks and steamrollers instead of doing the work?

We arrived at Albina – or what was left of it. Once a popular holiday resort for Surinamers, it was now a forlorn little township of prefabricated and wooden houses. The cabins looked deserted, the gardens dusty, neglected and sandy. We were on the banks of the Marowijne river, stretching wide and sluggish, opaquely brown with Amazonian mud, like all the rivers in Suriname. To cross the river into French Guiana there was a choice of motorised dug-out canoe or mini car ferry. Tickets to the ferry were in a small wooden building. It was filled with young men in ragged clothing who lounged on bare wooden benches, drinking coke as if that was all they had to do that day. Perhaps it was.

The ferry arrived and we drove on to it, together with two small trucks laden with sacks, another car and a motorcyclist. Chains rattled and the engine started up. We left Albina, stirring up the yellowy beige water as we went. Fat white catfish with giant whiskers ogled us from the mud as we left Suriname.

The journey took twenty minutes. The ferry drew into a smart little port, shining with white paint. Driving off the ferry we were saluted by two French gendarmes, resplendent in tropical whites and kepis. We blinked our eyes. In twenty minutes and the space of a brown river, we had crossed from the third world of Albina to the first world of modern-day France. Documents were efficiently stamped and we were courteously waved forward and out of the port area. Whereas in Albina the colour scheme had been brown, black, and grey, here suddenly, someone had readjusted the colour filters. From monochrome we had emerged into a Technicolor landscape of blue, white and golden sun. The roads were swept and smooth – and wonder of wonders, there were even white lines painted down the middle of the highways, a sure sign of prosperity. We hadn't seen those for months. What next?

'What next' was our little pension 'La Tentiare' in Avenue du President Franklyn Roosevelt – part of the penitentiary from the bad old days when French Guiana was a dreaded penal colony. A painted two-storey colonial building, all blue and white inside, ex-uded old colonial charm – as did the proprietors. We drove around the town, marvelling at the restored governor's house, the town hall, and the air-conditioned efficiency of the post office. This was a Département d'Outre-Mer of France, part of La Belle France and everywhere the pride of that fact was in evidence.

That night, after a good French meal in a little restaurant, where a raucous macaw oversaw the establishment, we crept under a blue and white embroidered counterpane. We were looking forward to the trips to Kourou and Devil's Island, and anticipating side trips to supermarkets and cold storage shops for French breads, Cam-embert, butter and coffee. That was one of the joys of a visit to French Guiana. We had to ask the question. 'Why?'

Why were these countries so contrasting? Why had the road to Albina degenerated into a morass of potholes? How could near destitution live so close to this efficiently functioning little outpost of the French empire? What had happened to Suriname?

It took time to put together any answers. People in Suriname spoke of the past rarely and never in detail. Perhaps they did not want to talk about it, or perhaps they assumed that everyone knew what had happened. Many of the answers to our questions re-volved around the figure of Desiré Bouterse.

Bouterse was a tall army officer with coal-black eyes, part Creole and part Amerindian. Initially popular and promising great things, he had seized power in the early 1980s and had imposed martial law in 1982. Members of the opposition were imprisoned and fifteen prominent citizens were executed in cold blood on the beach near Fort Zeelandia – among them the head of the main trade union, lawyers, academics and journalists. It was still spoken of with grief, anger, resentment, and bitterness, particularly by those who were related to the victims. There were rumours of widespread infiltration of the drugs trade in Suriname related to this period and spread over many sectors of society.

Old ghosts from Surinamese history walked again. Once more Maroons had taken up arms against authority. Under Ronnie Brunswijk, a Njuka Maroon, they rose up against the government in 1985, demanding elections, a free press and respect for Maroon sovereignty. They were the SLA – Surinamese Liberation Army – but were often called the JC ('Jungle Commando'). Bauxite production (eight-five per cent of the export trade) was disrupted. Bouterse retaliated, raiding villages where Maroon civilians were killed in large numbers. Ten thousand Maroons fled for refuge to French Guiana. The army then recruited one thousand Tucayana Amerindians to fight Brunswijk's Maroons. In the process the road to Albina was mined; hence the huge craters and potholes, and Albina itself was largely abandoned. The economy fell into disrepair. People told of going across the country to Guyana – or even to Miami – to buy basic necessities like flour.

In 1987 elections were held and the military wing was defeated. The other political parties, organised according to cultural groups, formed a ruling coalition under President Ronald Venetiaan. It was not until 1992 that a final treaty was negotiated, giving the government authority over the entire country, and honouring Maroon economic, political and cultural rights.

But nothing is ever quite final in Suriname. In 1994, just before we arrived, a hydroelectric plant with American connections was seized by an unknown group who demanded the resignation of the government and decentralisation of power. Government commandos freed the hostages. In 1995 there were riots in Paramaribo over food prices. The exchange rate had gone berserk and we noticed that every street trader could quote the international exchange rate day by day. Slowly, under the Venetiane government, inflation was brought under control. In 1996 violence almost broke out from Maroon and Amerindian denizens of the rainforests, angry at government granting of foreign logging rights.

In the 1996 elections, Desi Bouterse was back, campaigning for re-election despite his actions in the past. He had been living in the background behind high walls in a well-fortified riverside mansion on the outskirts of Paramaribo, reputedly surrounded by a caiman-infested moat. Campaigning involved generous gifts like outboard motors to rainforest communities, parties and T-shirts all round. On the night before the elections we listened to a huge NDP party happening loudly on an area of vacant land just down the road. Loudspeakers blared with plenty of speeches, bands, food and fireworks. His party, the NDP, won more seats than any other single party and a coalition government was formed. Since Bouterse knew he would be unacceptable internationally he took a back seat and Jules Wijdenbosch, a tall quiet man in spectacles, was put in as president.

From time to time we saw Desi Bouterse at an evening function. Dark suited, with opaque black eyes, surrounded by henchmen, he brought a brown aura of fear into the room when he arrived. Ronnie Brunswijk was also in evidence. He was in government now. He was also a fanatical football fan, a player, owner and manager of his team, and he had not forgotten his days of fighting in the forests. It is said that during one football match, he appeared with his gun, firing into the air, threatening to shoot any member of the opposing team who scored a goal – and *all* of his team if they lost.

'Suriname,' as the tall Dutch ambassador's wife said, 'may be a lot of things, but it is never politically boring!'

The rest of the visit to French Guiana pointed up the contrasts. The roads were wide, new and smooth, sweeping past plantations and small Maroon villages. In small thatched stalls made of tree branches Maroon handcrafts were sold, panels, trays and tables carved in intricate geometrical designs.

At Kourou, the European Space Centre was a huge, sleek and glossy implant into the tropical landscape. We were shown round with Gallic courtesy and thoroughness and the history and functioning of the Centre was explained in exhaustive detail. We had pouches of maps, statistics and – like the little boy who once borrowed a book on penguins from the library – we learned more about the launching of satellites into space than we had ever wanted to know or thought to ask. The question 'Why here?' was answered immediately – the nearness to the equator makes it possible to launch spacecraft with minimal changes to the trajectory, and the additional energy created by the earth's rotation at that latitude saves fuel and money and prolongs the life of the satellites. We saw the huge 'movie theatre', its screen a vast window encompassing the entire night sky, where invited guests can watch the launching of rockets – and vowed to apply for a ticket. We marvelled at the newest rockets standing on tiptoe, against the brilliant blue sky, waiting their turn to be flung into orbit, not in search of Valhalla but in the name of science.

And then there was Devil's Island. We had read *Papillon* by Henri Charrière. Who has not? Reading it, growing up in Australia, it seemed, as did so many books then, that I was reading about some country in a far universe, a place that was so far from the reality I knew that it hardly seemed to exist at all. Of course I would never go there. The possibility never even crossed my mind. And yet here we were. Now we were on the ferry to Devil's Island, the smallest of the 'Iles du Salut' the scene of one of the most savage penal colonies in written history, infamous for its rough justice and the brutal conditions of life, but a colony organised by one of the most cultured and sophisticated nations on earth. The lushly forested island came slowly into view, a hump of green. The ferry moored at the jetty. We watched a metre-long grey iguana, preening himself in the sun, like a guardian dragon. The prison buildings were still there, the stones glaring white and hot in the sun, now a resting place for sleepy lizards and tourists. The cruelties of the past, the gangs of sweating, half-starved mosquito-bitten men, forced to work half-naked in the blazing sun, are present only in the small museum and the imagination, and perhaps, to sensitive souls, in the vibration of memories imprinted on the earth itself.

The cemetery was humid and shady. Death in this steaming place must have seemed infinitely preferable to life. Small russet-furred agoutis scurried about, busy on agouti business among the gravestones. Birds chirped. We thought about Henri Charrière's escapes, and the Dreyfus case, about the string of escapees counting the 'seventh wave' as the sea crashed on to the rocks below; about the rare escapees who may have come to the border of Dutch Guiana (Suriname) only to be eaten alive by piranhas as they swam the Marowijne river. There are stories on record of Dutch guards on the Suriname side, who, hearing of escapees, would patrol the riverbanks waiting to hear the screams. Then they could go back to bed, relieved of the necessity of a rainforest pursuit. Some reached the forest, only to be set upon by hordes of army ants.

Suriname was a surreal posting, a place of fireworks, drug barons, jaguars and anacondas, a place where seven cultures mingled, a place where by crossing a muddy piranha-infested river one emerged from poverty to gleaming rocket science, the only place in the world where a trip to Devil's Island is seen as a holiday break for a long weekend.

4

Dancing with a Coffin

One day not long after the trip to French Guiana, KJ was about to leave his office. He looked across the road to the old cemetery. A funeral was entering the gate. He watched with increasing incredulity. As they carried the coffin, the pall-bearers were dancing, jumping and jiggling the deceased up and down, even bouncing the wooden box, throwing it up and catching it again. They wended their way down the track between the gravestones, hopping and gyrating as they went. Shaking his head in disbelief, KJ got into his car and went off to keep yet another ministerial appointment.

Suriname was like that. Not only did every culture have its own food, its own way of language and its own dances and costumes, but in the middle of daily life, one was constantly surprised by the streams of custom and spirituality that flowed beneath the outer lives of each group.

The dancing coffins were carried by men of the Maroon forest people. We asked a rainforest healer about it. He said: 'The people who dance with a corpse dance because it is a ninety-year-old corpse, the soul and spirit danced already happily to God.' Or perhaps, on a more practical note, it was a way of being sure that the person was truly dead.

The Maroons, the descendents of slaves who escaped in the seventeenth and eighteenth centuries, were one of the oldest and largest groups, and were a palpable presence in Paramaribo. There was constant coming and going between the city and their forest communities. Caged macaws and tiny monkeys were sold by forest people at the side of the road. There was a stall in the centre of town, near 'Pullapanty', where distinctive Maroon wooden panels and stools were for sale, carved in geometrical patterns, and where sometimes in traffic a 'tiger' or jaguar skin would be hanging in the sun. The Paramaribo zoo waged a sad war against marauders from the rainforest since captive animals made no sense to the bush people except as an easy source of food. Overnight, a capybara would disappear, or a dead flamingo would be found, reduced by morning to a few desolate pink feathers in a bucket. One of the first projects of the American Women's Club was a 'hunter-proof fence for the zoo'.

We were given an insight into this unique society, synthesised from the multiple traditions of seventeenth-century runaway slaves, and forged in the silence of the Amerindian forest into a new race.

Our teacher was Olof.

One day there was a ring at the front gate. On opening it I was confronted by a tall, broad-shouldered sweating Dutchman in rumpled clothes. He had red hair, a big, open, friendly face and said: 'Hi, I'm Olof Smit. Ernie B told me to come and cure your headaches.'

Ernie B was the Minister of Planning. He had suffered from crippling migraines for years, as I did. Olof had cured him with a series of his rainforest teas and body washes. Relieved of his pain, Ernie had become a fan of Olof. And, if there was the possibility of no more headaches, I was prepared to be a fan too.

In came Olof, wheeling his bicycle, and sat down on the veranda. He had been a Dutch film producer. While researching for a documentary on the food chain in Holland he was appalled by the farming practices he uncovered; in particular, the extent of the forced growth and factory farming necessary to achieve the astonishing agricultural yields for which Holland is famous.

'A country as small as Holland,' he said, thumping his fist, 'cannot produce that amount of food in any healthy way.'

Years ahead of his time, he became convinced that through over-farming and depletion of the soil, Europe was being fed without nourishment from plants and animals without soul. This, predictably, did not endear him to the Ministry of Agriculture or the Dutch Board of Tourism. Out of favour with the authorities, and

persona non grata, it was about this time that Olof met some Surinamers in Holland who suggested he should go to the rainforest
to learn how the bush people lived in harmony with nature. This
he did, living in the forest for five years. He apprenticed himself
to rainforest healers, spent time with them, and was sent foraging
alone in the depths of the forest to develop his own cures. He also
married Merre, a beautiful young woman from among the Maroon
people. The system of healing he learned involved 'Waka Waka',
or 'emotional cold' in the body, which can be interpreted as emotional barriers and their effects. In his own words, this is how he
explained the philosophy: 'A healthy human being is a person who,
from the beginning of her existence, knows harmony between cold
and warmth; warmth – in the sense of love, patience, tolerance
and care; cold – in the sense of barriers which have been imposed
on the child in the name of love, by his environment. Cold, like
warmth belongs in the body – together they create harmony in
the system. Cold and warmth are like positive and negative forces,
constructive and destructive, yin and yang, good and bad. They
need each other; one cannot exist without the other.'

If the warmth is blocked, the excess of cold has a free run. It
travels around within the system until it finally settles in the weak-
est parts.

The results of 'Waka Waka' take many forms, involving the
weak areas in the body where the travelling cold can settle and
harden. In the sinuses the cold gives rise to mucus, leading to infections, headaches and migraines. In the spine it can lead to herniated discs, and in the joints it gives rise to rheumatism. In the
muscles and nervous system blockages can also arise and, in the
cells, it is said that the cold can lead to various kinds of growths
and tumours. Therefore, the people of the forest say: 'It is of the
highest importance to save our children from "Waka Waka" by
raising them in harmony. In the case of illness it is important to
dissolve the cold in time with the traditional rainforest remedies.'

To begin the treatment Olof took out his giant pendulum, a
disc the size of a grapefruit, a slightly sinister object made of or-
ganic matter – skin? claws? bark? – and began to swing it slowly

on a leather thong. As it swung he asked questions, addressing the rainforest spirits – the 'Winties', 'Mother Earth' and 'Father God' – receiving answers, it appeared, about his client's life, motivations, and deep-seated reasons for the headaches. He nodded as he received the information, then turned and explained what he had been told.

As he focused on the swinging pendulum, I watched him. Somewhere in the back of my mind a picture formed of his massive, broad figure clad in the costume of a seventeenth-century sea captain, standing in front of a slave ship in full rig. Was it a vision of the past? A time warp? In another life, could Olof have captained one of the many slave ships that brought their cargo to Suriname? Was it possible he had been drawn back on a healing mission to the descendants of the people he had transported? Possibilities streamed across my mind. The picture vanished. We parted, with the promise that he would return with the course of treatment.

When the treatment came it was contained in a series of crisp, new brown paper bags. Each one contained an aromatic assortment of leaves, bark, wood-chippings and roots – all looking very much like garden sweepings destined for a bonfire. Each mixture was carefully assembled to cleanse different systems of the body – the blood, the nervous system, the digestive system – in an ongoing process. Each bag was to be boiled in a saucepan of water, strained into a tea and drunk three times a day. Some of them tasted pleasantly herbal, some like paint-stripper and some like cat's pee, but I drank them faithfully, regardless, and finished off with two 'washes' to be poured over the body after a shower. The rinses smelt as fragrant as expensive spa products.

I wish I could say that an instantaneous cure was achieved. It was not. We repeated the course, following it up with the juice of the 'bita wiri' plant (the well-named 'bitter weed') sniffed up into the nose, and designed to clear mucus from the body – which it surely did. We had visitors that day. They arrived just after I had sniffed up the burning plant sap from the palm of my hand. I talked to them red-eyed, and my nose streamed burning torrents for twelve hours. Bita wiri is a plant also known as 'lady of the night' – after dark its tiny white flowers emit a strong, heady perfume like sweet incense. Its small leaves are also used as a delicious green vegetable. From that day on, those would be its only functions in our house. No more medicinal use. Far too painful.

The headaches did not disappear immediately but abated in frequency and severity. The Winties communicated to Olof that the problem was no longer headaches, but 'the fear of headaches' – which had a ring of truth about it. They have continued to abate. Now there are none. Who knows?

Olof continued his research. One of his cures appeared to have success in restoring quality of life to children diagnosed as HIV positive. His 'black oil' worked wonders with bone and joint problems. He had success with some forms of rheumatism, with arthritis and with herniated discs. Sponsored by an American organisation he went on a lecture tour of naturopathic clinics in Florida, speaking about his work.

His young wife joined him on one of his visits to America. Brought up in contact with nature and fresh from the silence of the forest, her reaction to Florida was extreme and dramatic.

'These people are all ill,' she said, recoiling from the crowds.

One day, they went into a flower shop, filled with long-stemmed roses and cultivated blooms. Merre became faint with shock and had to go outside.

'All those flowers,' she said, 'they have no souls.'

Earlier spiritual traditions existed in the forest. Amerindian groups still lived in sandy forest clearings, walking softly barefoot. They slept on simple raised platforms under a rudimentary shelter made of poles and branches. Strangers who visited their clearings would find the space apparently deserted, unaware of the many eyes watching from among the trees. The Arawaks too had their deep connection with the profound silence of the forest, in their ceremonies, their visions, their powerful connection with nature spirits and their prophetic dreams.

Surinamese friends were visiting an Arawak community near the airport. There was a chance to join them. We were greeted by a small, square, stocky man with piercing black eyes and the strongest legs I had ever seen – like tree trunks growing from the earth. The people were formal and cautiously welcoming, but only because trusted friends were present. If they had not known us, the forest clearing would have appeared empty, and we would have been observed by unseen eyes. A gift of meat, which they could not normally afford, was accepted and served back to us, the givers, together with a tooth-breaking grainy disc of manioc bread and a minute quantity of wild green vegetables. We ate at midday, in stifling heat, sitting on rough wooden benches under a thin thatched shelter. The conversation was in Sranaan Tongo, translated for my benefit into English via Dutch. Talk was of a possible project to enable the community to sell their clay pottery and woodcarvings. A circle of carved poles stood in the compound, hinting at secret community ceremonies. The head of the family told the story of a dream encounter he had had with a being from another planet. A few sad, skeletally thin dogs crouched on the periphery, their eyes hungering for scraps.

After lunch the group were in a huddle, discussing projects in Dutch and Sranaan Tongo. Almost exploding with heat I wandered to the edge of the compound where the forest began. It looked cool so I ventured in a little way. The ground sloped steeply towards the sound of running water. I found myself in the midst of an enclosing world of tangled lianes, tree trunks, and dense-leaved shrubbery. For a while I sat with my feet in a small pool, wondering about leeches. There was no sound. No insects. No birds. Not a leaf or branch moved. The silence and stillness of the forest was intense, heavy and profound. It was unwelcoming – menacing, even. I got up to walk back up the incline, and realised that I had absolutely no idea what direction I had come from. A kind of mocking confusion seemed to overlay my brain; the Arawak settlement could have been anywhere. Truly at that moment I could have believed myself to have been bewitched in some way by malevolent spirits of the rainforest. Emerging into the yellow heat and sunlight, it was as if the entire land had changed. Heart pounding, I ran panic-stricken through long dry grasses which clawed my legs as I passed. I knew that if I called, my voice would not be heard and wondered if I would be found before heat exhaustion set in. And then, as suddenly as the state of panic set in it was over. I heard voices in the distance, and the settlement reappeared.

Shamans from elsewhere were attracted to the rainforest, hoping to learn from the old traditions. They too had their followers. Sometimes one or other of them conducted a workshop or trance session. These were often attended by some of the scores of earnest young Dutch and Belgian eco-warriors who trudged Suriname, hairy-legged and backpacked, eyes shining with zeal, usually working on developmental projects for 'Stichtingen', the equivalent of NGOs.

I joined one of these rainforest workshops. We were a motley crowd of eco-warriors, developmental workers, artists, lawyers, doctors, psychologists and even an accountant. Dusty, hot, sweating and unkempt, we sat in a circle on the ground around the buttressed roots of a vast kapok tree – the Tree of Life. The profound silence of the forest invaded our minds, stilling all speech. The texture of heavy heat and immense silence was overwhelming. It was like a blanket thrown over the senses to those of us raised in the battering noise of cities.

This particular shaman was Belgian, a small chubby man in a crumpled shirt and sarong. He had piercing, ice-cold blue eyes. His young wife, a beautiful big-boned Surinamese girl, sat passively on the outskirts of the group, observing the proceedings through hooded eyes while her two children played naked in the dirt, dragging thin, unfortunate puppies by the tail. When one of the children squatted in the dirt in the sacred circle, she took two leaves and reverently removed the small shit before subsiding again into heavy-eyed meditation. The shaman began his session, seemingly transported, as he worked himself into a state of ecstasy. Splintering the silence with wordless, tuneless chanting, he played on drums, bowls, bells, triangles and rattles, culminating with an ear-splitting blast from a ram's horn.

Underpinning the sometimes chaotic out-workings of this land of seven peoples was the deep and serious spirituality of all of the groups. Hindu temples arose in residential areas, some still in the process of being built by enthusiastic devotees. They were romantic fantasies in stone and cement, creations from a dream of Old India that none of the builders had ever seen. Their domes and arches, their fluted and twisted pillars, their elephants, tigers and lotus flowers, were at night the silent haunt of white owls.

The Hindu community was as vibrant in its spirituality as the Amerindians and Maroons. Temples were crowded, and the visit of a guru from India attracted wreath-bearing crowds of thousands. The Indian embassy's cultural centre taught yoga, music and dance to all who wanted to learn. Op weg naar zee, at the far end of the Kwartaweg, near the sea, was the place where Indian cremations were reverently held in the traditional manner. Holi was celebrated in the streets with coloured powder as. Vibrantly, as in India.

Because of my interest in meditation I had been 'adopted' by several members of the Hindu community, among them Kamla and Shakuntala who phoned one day to arrange a meeting. Two elegant Indian women in Western dress appeared for tea. A high-powered psychiatrist and a psychologist, they were friends, and were committed to an adventurous and eclectic approach to their work. Every year a stream of groundbreaking therapists came from Holland to Suriname to teach. At the same time they and their professional friends found no conflict between their professional work and their spiritual beliefs – rather, they mined their spirituality for ways to help their clients, and searched their professional knowledge for light on their spiritual tradition and practices.

One day the phone rang. In fact it rang several times. Each time the caller, including Shakuntala and Kamla, and my German artist friend Anita, enthused about a new technique of yoga breathing that had come to town. This was very Suriname. People tended to phone up out of the blue for no other reason than that they had heard that someone interesting was in town. One breathless message followed another all day: 'It's at 7.30 in such and such a hall, and you must bring a rug to sit on. I'll pick you up! You must come!'

After the fourth call it was irresistible. Of course I went along. We sat on the floor in a hot, humid hall, learning breathing techniques from a beautiful young sari-clad Indian woman. The technique was powerful. Even more striking was the enthusiasm and the response in Paramaribo. Obviously the phone lines had been busy. Our teacher from the Art of Living Foundation had expected to stay for two weeks and teach thirty or forty people. Such was the response and demand that she stayed in Paramaribo for three months, teaching more than two thousand people from every walk of life and from most of the cultural groups.

The Jewish community, too, had played a prominent part in the historical scene. Jewish settlers had been among the first to come. Fleeing the Inquisition, they moved on to Suriname when the Dutch were defeated by the Portuguese in 1654. They settled in the Jodensavanne, on the edge of the forest the scene of many slave escapes and revolts, those told in the Maroon stories of Fesitem – the stories of Ayako, Lanu and Seei, and their escapes to the Indians. Punishments for the escapees were appallingly severe in Suriname, ranging from whippings through to unspeakable tortures, but there is no record of whether the Jewish plantation owners were any harsher or more lenient than others. Sadly, it was the manner of the time.

The nineteenth century saw the end of worship at the synagogue of Jodensavanne, with a fire in 1860, though economic crises and slave revolts had caused the sugar plantations to be abandoned long before that. With the abandonment of the old settlement to the lianes of the forest, the Jewish community moved to Paramaribo, and the magnificent Neve Shalom (House of Peace) Synagogue was built. It is a baroque masterpiece in wood, next to the largest mosque in the Caribbean. The two coexist peacefully side by side, not even a fence between. Inside the synagogue, the multicoloured congregation walks silently on a floor covered with sand, a reminder of the Passover flight, and its forty years in the desert – and also, perhaps, a practical measure since a lighted candle, if dropped on the Sabbath, may not be picked up by an Orthodox Jew.

One day at the office KJ was thrilled to be approached by Rene Fernandez, a gentle man and a prominent member of the Jewish community. The EU had a cultural programme. Could it be used to provide some assistance in restoring the Neve Shalom Synagogue, as a heritage site? The project was presented and agreed, and piece by piece, this magnificent old building regained its gleaming white exterior, and the ancient interior – its bima, its balcony, its candlesticks and its roof beams once more glowed with pride.

And then there were the Christians. A quarter of Surinamese Christians are Catholic, and about one in five is Protestant. The churches were full on Sundays. In the course of duty we went to a variety of services. These might be taken in a mixture of Dutch or Sranaan Tongo. Surinamers tend to sing Germanic hymns in very four-square rhythms, in a surprisingly ponderous and un-South American style, but occasionally Sranaan Tongo would be used. The translations of scripture into this language were beguiling:

> *Wi tata na Hemel, joe nen moe de santa*
> Our Father in heaven, hallowed be your name
> *Joe kondre moe kon, Joe wani moe go doro*
> Your kingdom come, Your will be done
> *Na grontapoe so leki na hemel*
> On earth as it is in heaven

Thus begins the Lord's Prayer.

One Easter we were invited to a full-scale traditional celebration in a local church in which all possible smells and bells were liberally applied. When the time came to sprinkle the congregation with holy water, the water was solemnly carried around the church in a plastic bucket as, intoning, the lace-clad celebrant formally dipped what looked like a giant toilet brush into the bucket and thoroughly doused us all as he passed.

The Catholic Cathedral of St Peter and St Paul is claimed to be the largest wooden church in the Americas. Its immense yellow-painted gothic presence stands at the lower end of Gravenstraat. The story goes that the massive greenheart pillars holding up the roof had twisted with the weight of the roof, as successive bishops added more ornamental structures to the original design. A firm of Dutch architects was consulted. Their solution was to raise the roof, taking the weight off the pillars. They then departed for Holland. Six months later they returned to find, as they had thought, that the resilient greenheart pillars had recovered and straightened themselves, standing proud and tall as they had done when they were young tree trunks in the forest.

We normally went to the Santa Rosa English-language church, presided over by Father Esteban Kross, a small and lively Surinam-er, seminary-trained in Trinidad. He had a decidedly Portuguese cast of features, an infectious sense of humour and a magnificent baritone singing voice, and used both of the latter to good effect in church and out of it.

One day Esteban phoned to say he was putting on a concert in aid of church funds. Would I sing?

It had been some time since I had sung in public. Almost eighteen months, in fact. This was going to take some preparation. In addition, I had no access to a piano in Suriname, and no idea where one might be found. It's amazing what can be done with a CD, musical scores, a tuning fork and a glass. Every afternoon, when the staff had gone, I closed all doors in the hot reception room of the house and set myself to recapture Mozart's 'Alleluia' and 'Porgi Amor'. And some Celtic songs with harp.

The concert arrived. Preparations were not helped when the young Surinamese pianist earmarked as my accompanist, thought he could sight-read the music on the spot. He couldn't. Esteban had put together an eclectic programme. He himself played a Mozart fantasia on the piano, and strode about authoritatively as Verdi's Don Carlos, emoting dramatically in a register several tones too low for him. Several local choirs sang, there were local dancers, recitations and instrumental soloists. There was a break in proceedings when the conductor of a local orchestra couldn't be found because for some reason she had gone off to check whether her car was still where she had parked it. The final treat was a performance of Schubert's 'The Trout' by a local choir. We settled down to listen.

In einem Bächlein helle,
Da schoß in froher Eil
Die launige Forelle
Vorüber wie ein Pfeil

73

(In a bright little brook, a capricious trout swam happily, it shot past like an arrow.)

The well-known tale of the little trout, enjoying an innocent life, and the treachery of the angler who muddied the water to catch it, rippled and rollicked along.

We listened. And listened. And went on listening. There was not one 'Trout' but a whole school of them, an unending series of pastiches in the style of every composer known to Western musicologists.

As we sat in the stifling heat of the church that night, enduring this over-enthusiasm, I was struck by the bizarre surrealism of the situation. What were we doing here, in this colony of sugar plantations and the torture of slaves, this place of Amerindian mysteries and Winti rainforest spirits, this land of mangoes and pomerac, macaws, anacondas and iguanas, listening to eighteen different versions of 'The Trout' by Schubert? Looking around at the varied faces of the audience, I wondered what they were all making of it. No doubt every one of them was hearing a different concert, each version coloured by the genealogical inheritance and emotional experience of the listener.

Perhaps the tale of treacherous angler and innocent fish has been sung many more than eighteen times in Suriname, since the first ships sailed up the Suriname river, and the first cockaded and pomaded settlers stepped ashore to muddy the waters and betray the minds of the unwary inhabitants.

5

Mince Pies and Monsters in the Forest

Just back from London. This time I had brought a new word processor. I used to laugh at the concept of 'processing words' but not any more. This one not only processed words but enlivened the journey as well. The taxi arrived as usual, at 3.30, and as usual I hadn't had any sleep. By 5.30 we were at Heathrow tapping our feet by the as yet unopened VAT office, and by 7.30 I was lugging the new machine off the plane in Amsterdam and embarking on the long march to Gate D27 for Paramaribo.

The milling multicoloured crowds of Suriname began. The area was full of people struggling along under the weight of TV sets, stereos, and even a dozen garden rakes tied together with string. This time I was there with the best of them, in a more subtle, black briefcase kind of way. I found my seat and hoped, as we all do, that the next seat might be free. But two Indian ladies bore down. The younger of the two was wearing Western dress and looked fairly ordinary. Her mother, who was fated to sit next to me, was clad in full sari and dripping with gold jewellery, and seemed to have as many arms and legs as a dancing Shiva, all whirling and all carrying parcels and plastic bags. She tripped over everything in sight and fell into her seat. I flung myself protectively on to the little word processor in its black case, and physically lifted her rather large sandal-clad foot as it was about to descend on to the machine. Holding the ankle I said: 'No, sorry, computer' – firmly, in my best empire-builder's voice, buttressed by that empire-builder's conviction that anything said clearly and firmly in English will of course transcend all language barriers.

For the rest of the journey, after a few unconvinced half-smiles, I pretended to be busy with my book from the waist up, while being aware from the waist down of an ongoing battle for the couple of inches of space that separated the little machine from the lady's left foot. We wordlessly battled it out, playing footsie over the air miles with a bit of advantage gained during toilet breaks.

I seemed to have won 'The Battle of the Left Foot' since the machine arrived undamaged, but what is the best way to travel with such objects? A 'fragile' sticker might just invite dropping and pounding by baggage handlers having a bad day, and if it is actually labelled 'computer' it might find its way into that special channel marked: 'For the Boys!'

About four hundred dog chews came back in the luggage for Star. That could have been difficult to explain to customs. Star crept unnoticed into the bedroom and found the open suitcase. Alerted by the sound of a squeaky toy being chewed, I rushed to see what was happening and there was a happy dog on the bed with all his Christmases come at once. He was bizarrely chewing on a dog squeak in the shape of a human hand – the very picture of what a ferocious bull terrier is imagined to be. When all the treats were packed into his special high kitchen cupboard, this immensely strong thirty-six-kilo English bull terrier sat on the floor, and gazed upwards emitting pathetic little mouse squeaks of desire.

It was the cool season. Everything is relative. The temperature in the bathroom was below 30°C, which was a joy, and the sun was actually covered by cloud one day.

Surinamers, anxious to extol the pleasantness of the climate would say: 'Sometimes it goes down as low as 27°C at night!'

'Tell that to the BBC weather forecasters,' I thought. In England, the newspaper headline 'Oooh! What a scorcher!' comes into play when it gets to 20°C and the English strip off their shirts and fall to the ground as they expire with the 'heat'.

Christmas goodies also came back in the luggage. We had invited forty people for a traditional English Christmas meal. The invitations were all out, fetchingly hand-tied with red bows and little gold stars. A cooking marathon was under way – everything made from scratch, as it had been in Angola, since traditional English Christmas fare was not available at all, let alone ready-made – and why should it be? Dear Mabel contributed a Caribbean black cake, so laced with rum that it threatened to auto-combust.

1996 in our house was not the Year of the Dog, the Rat or the Horse, but definitely the Year of the Mince Pie – one hundred and forty-four of them. Even KJ got involved in the kitchen at night, spooning home-made fruit mince into the pastry cases and Star lived under the table waiting for scraps to fall. I swear his little brown eyes looked more like currants every day. We hadn't read then, that currants and raisins were potentially fatal for dogs. Perhaps it depends on the amount of dried fruit and the size of the dog.

An immense turkey was ordered and a ham, Christmas puddings were ready, Christmas cakes were made and decorated, little star and Christmas tree-shaped biscuits were stamped out. Christmas crackers were stuffed with special treats. And then with a week to go, a letter arrived from the Department of Foreign Affairs saying that it had been decided that 21st December was the date for the government dinner for the diplomatic corps, and would we please cancel ours.

For a while I was not amused and went around looking like Queen Victoria at her most purse-lipped. But we rallied and re-invited everyone for a modified Christmas tea on Boxing Day. The dinner was enjoyable, though a mite steamy and mosquito-ridden in the open air. The great Boxing Day spread looked like an illustration from a cookery magazine and was a huge success for those who could come. Eventually the turkey was consumed and met its predestined end in a fine soup. There is no point fighting these things. That is absolutely not what the job is about. Gracious capitulation was the only way and perhaps, who knows – the favour might be returned one day. It would be – in a rather more magnificent form than we could have anticipated.

After Christmas word came that German friends from Brussels would be visiting for a long weekend on the last leg of a trip to the Americas. They were the ideal guests. They had visited us in every country except Angola and were the only friends intrepid enough to venture to Suriname. They always arrived dressed in magnificently appropriate tropical outfits staggering under the weight of their telephoto lenses and carrying extra rolls of film wrapped in armour-plating, maps, pedometers, altimeters, guides and reference books. They would unpack and produce their plan of campaign for the holiday, and would depart each day in their hired car after breakfast, heading for the nearest supermarket for their lunchtime picnic. They would thoroughly explore mountains, caves, and sights all day, returning in the evening with their stories, their geological specimens and their collections of seeds, beetles and moths to look up in their reference books. Who could ask for better houseguests?

Playing the host in Suriname, however, was more of a challenge than in some other places. It was not the ideal place in which to entertain guests since the tourism industry and transport were still in rudimentary form. Remembering the exhortation we had seen for visitors to 'bring their own hammock' we put some thought into where they could go. The Jodensavanne was a must, and together we pottered around the old ruins and graveyard in the sticky silent heat, and let our imaginations embroider the past. We drove around Paramaribo to exclaim anew at the old wooden buildings. But we also wanted to do something different. Office staff recommended Cola Kreek, where Surinamers went to play at the weekend. We were assured it was a delightful spot, cool and refreshing. This was where everyone went with their families to have a good time, they said.

Cola Kreek was near the airport via the sleepy and dusty little town of Onverwacht. This unlikely little settlement seemed to be a major graveyard for abandoned trains, their surreal remains overgrown and peeping out of the bushes. It seemed that, like many schemes in Suriname, plans for a grand rail network had bitten the dust and everything had stopped dead right there at Onverwacht. Scratching our heads, as we often did in Suriname, we continued on.

Cola Kreek was well named after the much-loved drink. Its waters having flowed through the rainforest, they emerged the colour of a glass of Coca-Cola; soft, cloudy and brown with the peaty residue of rotting leaves. Through a grandiose gateway, the 'resort' itself was a large flat open area where streams were contained in rocky outcrops, and marshalled into a few shallow pools. A roughly built gazebo or two served as picnic shelters, and a few small children lolled in the puddles. Further upstream, in the forest, the water was deeper and shaded by trees, and more daring swimmers could paddle in the opaque brown water among thick waterweed and tiny darting tropical fishes. A tall, stick-thin man wearing baggy bright coloured shorts stood in the stream dragging a stick. He informed us that he was looking for gold. He still hadn't found any by the time we left. We wondered how long he would stay there. We drank some coke in celebration of its namesake and decided that the dubious charms of Cola Kreek must be directly related to the family parties, the jollity of the company and the excellence of the food and drink that people consumed there on Sundays.

Our next attempt to entertain our Germanic friends was a visit to Brownsberg Nature Reserve in the Brokopondo region about one hundred and thirty kilometres from Paramaribo. This, we were told, really was wonderful. There were small cabins to hire, and nature trails, and since it was five hundred metres high, the views were spectacular. We packed our picnic and set off in a borrowed four-wheel drive. This was just as well. Logging contracts had been given to a number of South East Asian companies. The virgin rainforest was being raped and gigantic trucks laden with huge slaughtered tree trunks were constantly lumbering along the road, tearing it up as they went. As we progressed further towards the park, the route degenerated into an area of ploughed earth, just two deep soggy wheel ruts separated by a high mound of earth. In places where trucks had turned to enter the rainforest, the ruts formed a grid like a giant game of noughts and crosses. Bucking as it went, the four-wheel-drive vehicle coped well in these conditions where a normal car would have been shipwrecked.

Having ploughed up the mountain to the high plateau, we found Brownsberg nature reserve deserted except for two forest rangers. Fat, green-clad and happy, they were dozing and chatting in plastic chairs in the shade, and managed to leave their conversation for just long enough to point to two wooden cabins perched on the very edge of a deep ravine. The 'rangers' looked sleepy and far from fit. We hoped not to need their services for any kind of protection or rescue operation.

The little wooden cabins were old, primitive and barely furnished. There was, as promised, running water of a sort, from rusty taps, there was electricity, and there were bunks with grimy brown canvas mattresses. It smelt mysteriously musty and there was a thick layer of dirt over everything we touched. But the view was wonderful – a little balcony overlooked a steep ravine, from which huge trees grew towards the light. We made tea and after a bit of wiping down, sat gingerly on the old wooden benches, looking into the treetops.

There were walks, we had been told.

'Brownsberg is the ideal spot to visit spectacular waterfalls!' said the brochure.

We set off to follow a trail. There was a waterfall depicted on the sign. The walk was said to take about an hour. We walked through well-defined bush trails. It was afternoon. No animals and very few birds stirred. The trail went on at an angle that was vaguely downhill but there was no sound or sign of a waterfall. Suddenly we found ourselves going down a slope so steep that our legs started running of their own accord. Grabbing trees to steady ourselves as we went, we reached the edge of a cliff and peered over. A perpendicular ladder made of branches lead down into the ravine. After some consultation we voted to go on. After all, we were so hot and tired now, we could hardly be more so, and we would be even more out of sorts if we turned back without seeing anything at all.

So we descended the ladder. It was intimidating but since it was impossible to look down, it was just a matter of holding on, looking forward to the spectacular waterfall and not thinking too much about the way back – but it did seem odd that there was no sound of water. When we reached the bottom we thankfully stepped on to flat ground and looked for the falls. The path stopped at a little pool. There was nowhere else to go. This must be the Surinamese version of a spectacular waterfall. It was, at most two metres wide, just big enough for four very hot people to sit in. There was a minuscule trickle of water oozing out of a rock and falling into the pool. We stripped to bathing suits and sat in the water, looking incredulously at the 'waterfall' and even more incredulously at the cliff-face ladder we would have to climb back up. We became aware of a certain amount of discomfort in our nether regions. A sort of prickling sensation. Hurriedly standing up we looked more closely at the pool. Dozens of tiny crabs were objecting to our presence by biting us vigorously on the bottom. There was nothing for it but to stop pretending we were enjoying ourselves. We splashed our bodies with water to cool off and set off back up the ladder. I don't remember much about the ascent except for an attitude of grim determination and a very firm grip. Four hot, grimy, dishevelled and disillusioned hikers finally stumbled into the cabin just as dusk was falling.

Grabbing the brochure, we re-read it. 'A good physical condition is recommended for participation in the sturdy hiking trip to the waterfalls of Brownsberg,' it said. They were not kidding.

We prepared some food on the rudimentary stove and sat on the balcony, enjoying the sounds of dusk, and talking. Birds were calling to each other, and there were rustles in the trees. We decided on an early night, since the other possibilities of entertainment were zero, and wearing as many clothes as possible in case, as seemed likely, some of the small and crawly Brownsberg fauna inhabited the old brown mattresses, we turned off the dim light and fell asleep.

At 2 a.m. we were awoken by the most astonishing noise. It was unlike anything we had ever heard. It was as though a hundred dragons were roaring and wielding chainsaws, just outside the window, accompanied by a hundred ogres playing gigantic pipe organs. The noise swelled and harmonised, booming, thundering, and echoing for miles, it seemed, through the treetops. There seemed to be many voices, many parts, many creatures – but what were they? How could any animal make such a noise? Were we being invaded – by what? Were they going to attack us? It was a primitive and terrifying sound, and I found myself reverting to the state of primal fear of a Stone Age man threatened by wild beasts at the door to his cave. Used to being more or less in control of a well-ordered household, it was as if everything I had ever learned disappeared – flooded out of my being by this gigantic cacophony. And there was nowhere to go. The danger was directly outside the flimsy hut, perhaps on the balcony itself. The only thing to do was to cower under the bedclothes and pray.

We listened, quaking, for as long as the noise went on. And eventually it trailed off, booming off into the distance in a series of directionless diminuendos. White-faced, we got up and went to find our German friends, hoping they might have a Germanic and rational explanation. Equally white-faced, they did not.

It was not until we arrived back in Paramaribo the next day that we found out what we had heard. No one had thought to tell us about the troupes of red howler monkeys that inhabited the Brownsberg forest.

These little creatures are neither dragons nor giants. They are no more than sixty centimetres in height, with the same length of tail. With their ruff of red hair they look like Snow White's seven dwarfs. Their call is one of the loudest in the animal kingdom and the sound can travel one and a half kilometres. Since they don't like conflict, their purpose is to warn other troupes of their presence and intimidate them without a confrontation. No wonder the sound inspires respect in other monkeys. Had I been in a tree I would have fallen out of it with sheer terror.

At the end of their short but adventurous visit, our friends were ready to catch their plane, but Suriname had another surprise for us. Our visitors had been told there was no need to reconfirm their flight, as it had already been done in Los Angeles. Unfortunately no one had told Suriname Airlines. On arrival at Johannes Pengel airport we found that our friends had been bumped off the flight during the weekend. This, for any travellers, would be a disaster. For our German friends, who prided themselves on their supreme organisation and booked all their travels two years in advance, it was a major trauma. There ensued a very Surinamese scene as, on the one hand, smartly suited airport executives assured us that all would be well, while on the other, all their friends, sisters and cousins and aunts who had been on standby, were quietly tiptoeing on to the plane via a side door. True to form, at the last minute two places were found at the cost of much nervous energy. We had learned to say 'This is Africa' and, in Angola, 'E Assim' – 'That's the way it is!' Now we were learning to say: 'This is Suriname.' I am not sure that our German friends ever learned to say it or indeed, ever forgave us.

Returning to normal life after these adventures, we found an invitation to another concert had arrived. Musical life in Paramaribo was mostly home-grown, with events put on by one or other of the different cultural groups, or do it yourself events such as the concert in the Santa Rosa Church. Once or twice, the pupils of a local music teacher gave a small concert. There were one or two talented teenagers among her pupils, who liked to play ambitious works like Liszt's 'Hungarian Rhapsody' very fast, with tremendous panache, and a lot of wrong notes. These could all be interesting, but just occasionally I found myself longing for a chance to sit and listen to some classical music beautifully played, without the need to either perform myself or cater for the evening. Every so often a poster would appear on a wall in town, which, when I had laboriously deciphered the Nederlands, implied that six months before there had been a concert in town and, of course, we had missed it.

My lively friend Solange, the wife of the Venezuelan ambassador, announced proudly that a Venezuelan pianist was coming to Paramaribo. Solange was a beautiful, witty young woman and a remarkable organiser. A large gymnasium was hired for the occasion and the only known grand piano in the city was borrowed and even tuned. There was great excitement at this rare event and the hall was full of expectant people, gentlemen gently sweating into the collars of their smart-casual shirts, and ladies making themselves even hotter by energetic fanning with the programmes.

It was so hot that the pianist's fingers began to slip on the keys. The concert paused and to general approbation and applause a huge and powerful air conditioner was wheeled on to the stage. It stood at the side, emitting a whirr and a blast of air that immediately blew the music off the piano and caused the row of potted palms on stage to bend and sway as if they were in a tropical storm. With steely concentration the handsome young pianist continued with his programme of elegant and delicate Venezuelan waltzes. To mark the occasion, the Venezuelan embassy had hired a cameraman to film the concert. He and his camera were mounted on one of those trolleys that are always used to film galloping horses in Hollywood movies. He was solemnly and silently driving himself up and down behind the potted palms, gliding smoothly as if without feet, appearing and disappearing between the plants as they waved in the air-conditioned hurricane. Every so often his head and his little red light materialised spectrally just over the pianist's shoulder. It was probably the most distracting concert we had ever attended. The music was enchanting, but the only way we could listen to it without giggling was by firmly closing our eyes.

At about the same time the American ambassador announced that he and his mature and lively wife were to be transferred from Suriname. The ambassador whom we will call Roy was a jolly bon viveur whose dinner suit had a tendency to give up and pop in despair. His sensible wife had been known to effect expert emergency repairs by winding a black cotton thread to and fro between the buttons. He was an entertaining raconteur and had the endearing ability to tell a story against himself. Our favourite concerned his time in South America. He had been seated at a very grand and very official banquet. Having spoken to the guest on his right for a while, he turned to the distinguished-looking man on his left.

'Hi,' he said, American-style. 'I'm Roy, from the American embassy.'

'My name is Placido,' said his neighbour. 'Placido Domingo.'

'Oh,' said our affable friend Roy. 'And what do you do?'

It is not on record whether the stunned Placido Domingo stammered that he 'sang a bit'. But to do him credit, Roy always finished the story by saying affably:

'Waal, waddya expect? Ahm a country and western man mahself!'

Like many of their other good friends we wanted to invite them for one last dinner before they went. The guest list was carefully planned, with a mixture of career diplomats, Surinamese friends and some of the friendly local honorary consuls. The menu was carefully planned too, finishing with home-made multicoloured fresh fruit ice creams in a glass. It was all supervised and served to perfection by the redoubtable Orlando, of the Keurslager catering company, and his cheerful and friendly team. Orlando was a large young Surinamer of African extraction, who combined the culinary skills of a chef with the deftness of a head waiter and the lightness of a dancer as he moved around the table. The setting looked splendid, silver and glass glinting among three flower arrangements proudly culled from the garden. There were fourteen people present. HQ had only provided a table to seat twelve, but with the judicious co-operation of a back-street carpenter we had managed to insert an extra wooden leaf in the centre and we were pleased with our enterprise and thrift.

That night there was a cold soup starter, the fillet steak was cooked to perfection, and the ice creams were served at exactly the right temperature – not in tongue-freezing frozen lumps, and not melting into a liquid; always an achievement in a hot climate. I sat back feeling pleased. For once. It had been a perfect dinner. The guests were finishing their last glasses of wine and conversation was flourishing in a pleasantly replete sort of way.

As I idly watched, two of the honorary consuls were engaged in a serious and absorbing political discussion. It reached its peak and they each leant on the table to emphasise a point. There was a loud crack. The table dipped in the centre and broke neatly like a communion wafer. Flowers, glasses and plates all slid with hypnotic slowness towards the centre as the centre of the table subsided towards the floor. Everyone watched with horrified fascination, unable to say a word. The French ambassador forgot his Gallic shrug and grabbed a few wine glasses as they slid past him. No one made a sound until the earth stopped moving. Then from her place at KJ's right the voice of the US ambassador's wife piped up: 'Will somebody move this table? It's restin' on mah knees!'

I looked at the scene. It looked like a Hogarth picture of the aftermath of an orgy. It was too good to miss. I got up from the table and dashed into the bedroom, reappearing with my camera. Lining up the carnage in the viewfinder to take this once in a lifetime shot, the funny side of it struck me and I started to giggle. The laughter spread down the table, and like all good jokes, grew to the stage where we were crying with mirth and holding on to each other. Orlando and his merry team heard the shrieks of laughter and peeped around the door to see what was going on. They joined in as well and fell about with us until everyone was exhausted.

By some miracle only two glasses were broken. Which was just as well, since replacements would have to come from Brussels or London.

The next day a letter arrived from the American embassy with thanks for 'one of the most memorable farewell dinners we have ever attended'.

As Christmas approached, Suriname once more geared up for the annual fireworks display. Dozens of container-loads of fireworks were imported from China. Shops with names like 'Bombel Paradijs' sprang up overnight. People who were poor for most of the year, saved up to buy enough pagaras, Catherine wheels and rockets to have a really good night. So good that every year several old wooden houses went up in smoke. Pagaras were the strings of stubby red crackers that went off like ammunition and frightened us in our first year in Paramaribo. Their original purpose was to clear out any bad energy or spirits from the old year and frighten away demons. This year the Dutch ambassador resolved to have the best ever New Year's party and invited everyone to watch him go down in history. He had fireworks set off from barges on the Suriname river and a string of pagaras one hundred metres long. His staff had been working for days to create this once in a lifetime display. We stood in the warm tropical night and emitted 'aahs' at the stars and palm trees reflected in the river. Then the bangs began. They were deafening. We put our fingers in our ears. The smoke began to drift. We were enveloped in a dense cloud of stifling smoke like a volcanic eruption and the entire party fled from the embassy on to the road outside to escape the fumes. There were no guests left at the end – and certainly all the demons must have gone as well.

Our friend Roselyne was also having a party. She was a glamorous and sultry ex-nightclub singer and fire-eater with a heart of gold. She was also the Colombian consul. We drove to join them the following night. Her Chinese husband was an importer of fireworks. The entire house and garden was wired up as a pyrotechnic display. Their neighbour, too, was having a party. Every time a rocket, a Catherine wheel or an exploding sun went up in one house, an answering salvo came from next door. It was like the finale of the '1812 Overture' in sound and light. The display went on for more than an hour until the garden and fence-posts were full of spent smoking sticks and every bird for miles around had departed. Satiated, we drove home, watching, as we went, as the sky lit up all over Paramaribo like a pre-enactment of Armageddon.

Word began to come from HQ about a possible transfer in the New Year. There were rumours that Trinidad might be available. KJ had already visited it to plan some regional projects but now before anything became official we wanted to pay a brief holiday visit just to see what it might be like. We would spend a few days in Tobago and a few days in Trinidad. Tobago was – and is – the island paradise of the pair. Robinson Crusoe is reputed to have landed here and well he might have done. In beaches and bays all around the island fine white sand gleamed and palm trees swayed. We glimpsed the rainbow gleam of a motmot bird's plumage in the garden, and ate crisp flying fish for breakfast, freshly caught and fried.

Trinidad, on first acquaintance, was unpromising, as we drove in from the airport through a light industrial area. The landscape looked dry, the buildings were haphazard and ugly and everything was, well, a bit messy. Looking to the right beyond the factories, we could see a range of green mountains in the centre of the island. They looked promising. We went over the Lady Young Road and stopped at a magnificent lookout where the city buildings and the harbour spread out in front of us. A raffish calypso singer in a straw hat attempted to serenade us with impromptu lyrics and a cheeky grin. We swept into the city, and booked into the up-side-down hotel – the only Hilton in the world where you catch the lift down the side of a mountain to the 'upper' floors. Treading carefully, we met the Head of Mission there, whom KJ might – just might – replace but no one was saying anything.

We were taken on a dizzying tour of the island, to see the Savannah – the fifteen-hectare green park in the centre of the city, around which all traffic revolves in endless clockwise circles. We gasped at the 'magnificent seven' – huge mansions from colonial times built in dreamlike fantasy styles. We were whisked to Maracas beach to try shark 'n' bake, fish, freshly fried, and served in a fried bread dough that puffs up to twice its size. Smiling owners of tiny stalls called Richard's, Maisie's, Molly's, and Sam's all vied for our custom, laying out tables of freshly prepared sauces to 'spice up de fish'.

We saw the Oval, beloved by cricket-loving Trinidadians, and the yacht club, where we ate flying fish again. We were shown the Pan Yards – steel pan band headquarters, which seemed to be full of metal frames, which we didn't really understand. People talked about Carnival, and tried hard to explain Trinidadian phrases like 'wining' and 'liming'. We went to visit the 'Long Circular Mall' – a logically impossible concept but a shopper's paradise after three years in Suriname. It was full of clothes made by local designers, imported china, a food hall selling steaming spicy Caribbean dishes, and shops full of brightly coloured West Indian sweets.

We were invited to spend the last two nights at the home of the German Head of Delegation. The house was one of the old, traditional Trinidadian wooden homes, built like a large gingerbread house in a green, well-treed garden. Behind its white wall a drive swept around the garden through a small porte cochère.

Our host lived alone. We met Beverley Anne Ho, his housekeeper, a cheerful soul, of Amerindian and Indian descent, proud of her position and prancing with delight at her own cooking – 'My cha cha chicken!' The fried chicken in breadcrumbs had cha cha'd perhaps too many times for its own good, and any crispness it had ever had had been well extinguished with a heavy brown sauce. Beverley gaily dumped the dish on a tablecloth that was clean but had never seen an iron, and left us to serve ourselves. I eyed the table arrangements speculatively, calculating the number of woman-hours of training that might be needed were Beverley and I to work together in the future. If we were transferred here would she take her place in the lineage of Thembeni, Bona and Gloria from Swaziland, Jane from Zimbabwe, Conceicao and Senhor Cruz from Angola, Mabel and Sarinah in Suriname? Or not?

We had lived and worked with so many people in so many places. We had become used to so many forms of address. In Swaziland, in the late 1970s we were 'Boss and Madam'. In Zimbabwe, it was Boss and Madam again, though it could be a hard struggle to prevent older workers from addressing KJ as 'Master'. In Angola, we were known as 'O Senhor Embaixador' and 'Senhora Dona Pamela'. Back in Swaziland, with more modern times, 'Boss' still applied, and 'Mnumzane', but I also answered to 'Mrs Pamela', 'Mayi' and sometimes 'Mother'. In Suriname we metamorphosed into 'Mijnheer and Mevrouw'. Here in Trinidad, what would it be?

We soon had our answer. After the tour of Trinidad we went into the kitchen. Beverley greeted us: 'You guys going for a swim?' she asked. This was Trinidad.

The morning, after the cha cha chicken, we came down to the kitchen hoping for breakfast. It was 31st August 1997. Beverley emerged from behind the refrigerator door and announced in a sepulchral voice: 'Princess Diana is dead!'

Like most people in the world who heard that news for the first time, our minds refused to believe it. Shaken, we made for the TV room hoping it was not true. Having followed the ups and downs of that beautiful young woman, as had the rest of the world, it was hard to believe that her shining presence and the much-photographed radiant smile had been extinguished overnight.

'Where were you when you heard about Princess Diana's death?' would become as memorable as, 'Where were you when you heard about Kennedy's assassination?'

For us, this death out of nowhere would always be associated with that sunny morning in Trinidad. Like Diana, Trinidad shines, it is a place of smiles, fun, colour and attraction, but, as in Diana's life, we would find that the sun that shone on Trinidad could also cast long, dark shadows.

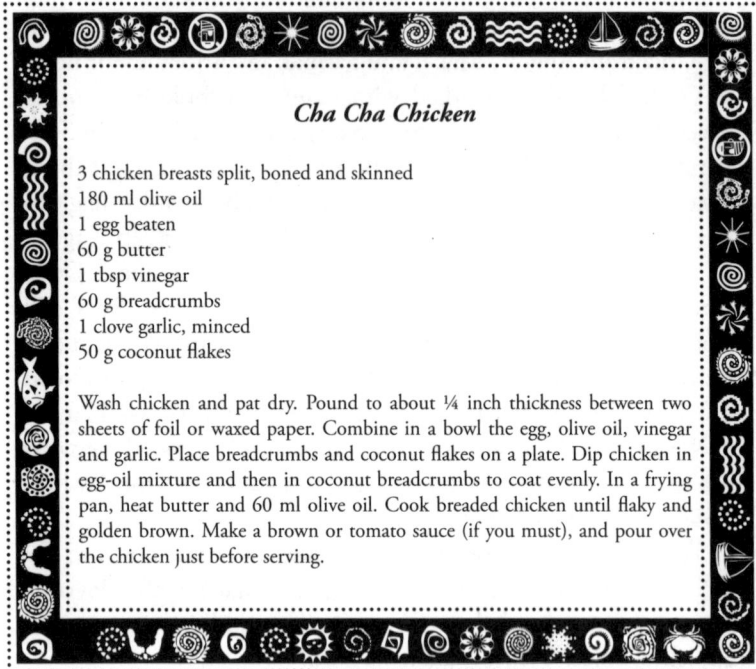

Cha Cha Chicken

3 chicken breasts split, boned and skinned
180 ml olive oil
1 egg beaten
60 g butter
1 tbsp vinegar
60 g breadcrumbs
1 clove garlic, minced
50 g coconut flakes

Wash chicken and pat dry. Pound to about ¼ inch thickness between two sheets of foil or waxed paper. Combine in a bowl the egg, olive oil, vinegar and garlic. Place breadcrumbs and coconut flakes on a plate. Dip chicken in egg-oil mixture and then in coconut breadcrumbs to coat evenly. In a frying pan, heat butter and 60 ml olive oil. Cook breaded chicken until flaky and golden brown. Make a brown or tomato sauce (if you must), and pour over the chicken just before serving.

6

The Road to Trinidad

It was confirmed. We were off to Trinidad. At last – a Caribbean country with real beaches, palm trees and even some glossy pharmacies as well. As usual, the farewells began. This time they took some unusual forms. The Scottish Dancing group held a 'Scottish dancing evening' with not only our favourite foods but our favourite dances as well. We all counted 'een, twee, drie, vier', collided and danced 'The Flowers of Edinburgh' for the last time. The Chinese ambassador held a karaoke evening for us and astonished us all by throwing his head back and singing karaoke Chinese opera for a very long time, in a very loud tenor voice. The lady chief of protocol sent an invitation to morning tea, at which I was presented with a gold necklace containing the Koebi stone (a white balance stone from the head of a carp, reputed to give 'balance' to those who wear it). Then we all linked hands and solemnly sang 'Auld Lang Syne' in Dutch. Solange cooked a special Venezuelan brunch with corn-bread arepas and white cheese. Even the friends of the forest shaman met for a farewell Indian meal.

But the biggest surprise of all came for KJ, with a summons to Foreign Affairs. We duly turned up, to find quite a crowd gathered. Speeches were made, and the president ceremoniously presented him with the 'Grootlint in de Ere-Orde van de gele ster' – the 'Grand Order of the Yellow Star', Suriname's highest honour. Standing draped in his red and yellow sash, he did look (as people wearing decorations always do) a bit like a Christmas parcel, but he felt proud, touched and highly honoured. Not the kind of thing one can wear very often, but on the rare occasions when he sports the tiny red and yellow lapel pin, he rather enjoys watching 'establishment' people eyeing it and wondering just what it is. (It was, of course, recognition for all his hard work, but I have always wondered whether my acceptance of the cancelled Christmas party might have biased Foreign Affairs just a tiny bit in his favour!)

While all this was going on, the packing and throwing out was happening. Tenders were put out for transport companies, and travel documentation had to be attended to. We took Star to the vet for his health certificates and found, to our horror, that Trinidad, as an ex-British colony, insisted on six months' quarantine for dogs. Poor Star. He had already done six months and more in a quarantine kennels in Britain before flying out to Suriname. Six months in a dog's life is equivalent to three and a half years in human terms. He had never left the garden in Suriname; even the vet did home visits. Was he to be put through all this trauma again? Why? Having shouted at KJ for accepting Trinidad, thrown a tantrum and wept in the toilet, I began to explore all possible options.

The government vet, who happened to be Star's vet, our dear Dr Ram Kaloop, was initially hopeful. He thought optimistically that if he wrote a letter underlining the fact that Star had never been in contact with other dogs, and that in addition his state of health was such that he would not survive quarantine well, the government vet in Trinidad would listen, as one professional to another. Word came back that government vet or not the rules were the rules. Dr Ram Kaloop was furious. The new American ambassador mentioned that when in Guyana, he had organised for his dog to be kept in private quarantine in the grounds of the American embassy. This was put forward and the suggestion was turned down. At Mabel's suggestion I thought about contacting a Guyanese fishing boat and sailing with Star and a friend to a remote part of the Tobago coastline. My German friend Anita was game for the adventure. A friend who was an ex-marine offered to do a parachute jump with Star strapped to his chest. I visualised squashed dog. The ideas grew wilder and wilder.

KJ was optimistic. He was confident that with all his experience and contacts, once he was there he would just see the Minister for Agriculture, have a word, and somehow all would be well. It was arranged that he would go on three weeks ahead to smooth the way. Star and I would follow, with Mabel and Anita. They would both come for two weeks to see Trinidad and to help with the unpacking. Mabel was thrilled. She had never been to a Caribbean island. Sarinah was not interested – she was looking forward to retirement with her daughter in Holland.

With Mabel, Sarinah and Anita and a bit of sturdy help from Olof our big healer friend, the packing was done. When we were taking up the karakul rug from Lesotho we found a thick layer of dust and fluff underneath it. In Paramaribo dirt and dust infiltrated the house in industrial quantities – probably because there was so little rain and so little grass on the street verges. We all stood gazing at the underfelt of dustballs and pussycats underneath the rug. Quiet little Sarinah stood with us. She was responsible for cleaning. We all looked at her meaningfully. Suddenly a mischievous expression crossed her face. For the first and only time in her employment with us she spoke up.

'Oh no! Mijnheer,' she said, pre-empting possible blame. 'That dirt is not from Suriname. It is from Africa. You brought it with you! Now you can take it away again!'

Star rushed about excitedly taking things out of boxes and running off with them. Every time we had moved there was more to pack, more to throw out and give away. Anita took one look at the clothes I was leaving behind, swept them up for herself and sent her clothes to the charity shop instead. She also blew apart my system of packing boxes for specific rooms. She went round searching for unrelated objects that could be squeezed into odd corners. For weeks after arrival I would find knitting inside kitchen saucepans and pyjama pants wrapped around glass vases. Remembering other packing experiences, we were extra careful. We thought optimistically that this time there would be no missing items. We sealed every box, packed every piece of electrical equipment and guarded all the doors. After the van left, Star and I stayed for three weeks in the empty, echoing house, still bizarrely home, but now populated only by the phantom presence of past happiness.

Word came from KJ that he was powerless to prevent Star from going into a pointless six-month quarantine. This beloved dog, who had lived in air conditioning, and was vaccinated to the eyeballs, was suspected of carrying some unnamed disease which might infect the multitudes of uncared for strays that roamed the streets of Port of Spain. They couldn't be serious!

Star was so happy in those weeks of packing. He enjoyed the excitement. On the day we left little Sarinah hugged him hard with tears in her eyes as she said goodbye. I loved and hugged him all the way to the airport, and felt like a traitor as I popped him into his travelling cage and slipped a tranquiliser into his mouth. He gave me a puzzled look. At Piarco airport we heard distant barking. We found ourselves waiting at the cargo terminal at 11 p.m. Finally we spotted Star on an open trailer in his box, being hauled with agonising slowness around the perimeter road of the airport, little white face peering anxiously out through the wire grille. That road will forever be known to us as the Star Trek. A Trinidadian customs official informed us that we would all have to wait in the airport until morning since we did not have form C63 among Star's sheaf of documents. Who had ever heard of form C63? What was it? Our first but not last encounter with the strange malady of officiousness that seemed to afflict bureaucrats in this otherwise kind and laid-back Caribbean paradise.

Some time after midnight the problems were solved. Star was met by some sinister-looking representatives from the quarantine kennels and we accompanied him to what would be his prison for the next six months. He was released into a small pen, and lay on a concrete floor that smelt of Lysol and urine. The heat was stifling. He looked ill and unhappy. I was overcome with guilt and despair. How could I explain what was happening to him? Heartbroken, hot and exhausted, we had to turn our backs after one last hug and leave him there as we went home to bed.

The first sounds the next morning were raucous shouts of green parrots as they flew into the tall palm trees of the Wildflower Park. The second sound was the call of the yellow Kiskadee – thought by the early French settlers to be saying 'quest-ce-que tu dis?' (what are you saying?) – and the third was the sound of the colony of long-tailed yellow and black Oropendola birds who lived in the huge Samaan tree of our next-door neighbours. The fourth sound was Mabel in the kitchen making Beverley's acquaintance, and beginning a two-week instruction course on her perception of Mijnheer and Mevrouw's likes and dislikes. As I walked to and fro in the house I would see them together, heads bent close, and hear snippets like 'Mevrouw likes the socks folded this way, in a little ball!' and 'Mijnheer likes to rest after lunch. You must all be very, very quiet.' But by far the best snippet concerned papaya.

For the past three years we had had a slice of papaya with a slice of lime or lemon every day as a lunchtime dessert. It was delicious; it was fresh and ripe – almost warm from the tree – and I had discovered that the alternatives, apart from Sarinah's apple fritters, were too dreadful to contemplate, being mostly pink or green ready-mix concrete of some kind. KJ murmured occasionally about it, but papaya it was. However, he had been thinking wistfully that with the transfer to a new country he would be reprieved from his daily slice of papaya, and might actually get something else for lunchtime dessert. Little did he know! As I walked through the kitchen carrying a packing box I overheard Mabel saying earnestly to Beverley:

'You must have papaya for Mijnheer every single day without fail. Mijnheer *loves* papaya!'

Beverley had greeted us with delight.

'I was hoping you guys would be coming. I thought you were nice people!'

'No pressure there then,' I thought. I will just have to get those tablecloths starched and ironed while staying 'nice'. And, looking at Beverley's black leggings and capacious T-shirt, find someone to make a working uniform as well.

On the first afternoon we set off to see Star, the first of the daily visits that would go on for six months. He was near Piarco airport, half an hour's drive past the Upside Down Hilton, over the Lady Young lookout point and then along a road used by Trinidad Maxi Taxis. These were minibuses with names like 'Elijah' and 'Halleluiah', in rampant competition for passengers, which dived and darted between the traffic. It was a challenging ride, as they sped past, soca music blaring, and passengers bulging from every window. I looked out speculatively, calculating my chances of mastering this style of driving or at least defending myself in the middle of it.

The quarantine kennels were in Curepe, a bustling, rough, busy area with frighteningly deep storm drains. It was full of small shops, small businesses and small houses which often combined the functions of both, with signs for lawyers, dentists, and dressmakers all by the same front door. A tiny stall near the kennels was hung with fruit, and sold the smallest and sweetest finger bananas on the whole island. The quarantine staff who had looked so sinister the night before transmuted by daylight into pleasant, gentle Caribbean men wearing cut-off trousers and Rasta hair. The piratical mode was just what the chaps were wearing in Port of Spain that year. Star was still bewildered but livened up when he saw us. He tried to perform his circular mad-fit of welcome in the confined space, cannoning into the concrete walls. His neighbour was an even sadder hound imported from England to go hunting small animals for 'bush meat'. We hoped they might cheer each other up a bit.

On our first weekend, Beverley suggested a picnic. She knew all the beaches in Trinidad, she said, and would come with us to show us the way. We believed her. On Sunday morning we packed a cool box and off we went, out towards the airport and then turned south. In Trinidad, people go 'to South'. The southern town, San Fernando, has a large Indian population. We saw the same impressive palmed, columned and walled white mansions belonging to the wealthy Indian population that we knew from Suriname. We drove on, beyond San Fernando, into country areas, where the houses were small and haphazard, where tethered cows grazed by the side of the road, goats and donkeys wandered, and people at roadside fruit stalls gazed incuriously as we went past. As we passed one of the fruit stalls, Mabel, ever watchful, said: 'Stop!' She dived out and came back with a round pumpkin-like object. Inside there were orange segments with a chewy texture and a taste like peaches crossed with French perfume.

'It's Mamasipote,' she said.

The drive seemed endless. We began to pass beach areas. Beverley dismissed them.

'Carry on!' she said.

We came to an area where the shore was one long plantation of coconut palms.

'This is Myaro,' said Beverley.

It looked shady and we were ravenous. We pulled the car up under the palms and got out. The beach was narrow, dropping from a low shelf into an area of dingy sand and seaweed. KJ and Anita decided on a swim before lunch. The rest of us were content to paddle. The two swimmers set out, swimming strongly and ducking under the waves. They seemed to be enjoying themselves and I began to unpack the picnic. The next time I looked they seemed to be a long way out, their heads bobbing beyond the small breakers. After a while I glanced again. They were still in much the same place, but further over to the right. We chatted and waited. Mabel was paddling in her bathing suit and giggling when the waves came up to wet her pants. Finally, the two swimmers came back in to the shore. They clambered out breathlessly, shouting to Mabel: 'Get out! Get out of the water! It's dangerous!' We stared at them.

'There are rip tides out there,' said KJ. 'We were carried out and couldn't swim against the current. The only way we made it was to lie on our backs and let the waves bring us back in to shore!'

Seeing KJ lying on his back, Anita had done the same.

'He's not worried,' she thought. 'Why should I be?'

He had been saying some last farewells under his breath.

As they sat there recovering a tall, gaunt fisherman walked past on the shore, swinging a bundle of nets.

'Don't you be swimmin' here now!' he called. 'Them waves, they carryin' you out for so!'

We looked at Beverley. She was eating a chicken leg, unperturbed by the fact that the new ambassador for the Commission of the European Communities had nearly perished in the first week of his posting. She had nearly succeeded in drowning her new employer.

The next days were spent unpacking boxes. Transferring a life from one country to the next always holds surprises. Perfectly

functioning lamps and electrical goods die in transit, another forty-five metres of electric cable and fifty plugs are necessary before
anything will work, and the tea towels have all mysteriously disappeared. The wooden cat that got lost among the shredded paper
every second move might choose to reappear – or not. This time
there were no breakages. Even the two treasured fish tank cabinets
from Suriname arrived safely and were standing ready to become
living jewelled mini-theatres once more. We began to think we had
finally solved the problem of how to control a move. Until, that is,
we unpacked the small stereo system. Anita and I had spent a long
time fitting together the polystyrene jigsaw puzzle and putting it
into its box. We had sealed the box with tape and wrapped it again
in brown paper to be sure. We had then placed the sealed box in
the locked main room to be taken directly in to the van. Now the
parcel seemed suspiciously light. Inside there were two speakers
and no music system. Somehow the music centre itself had performed a Houdini act.

We had indeed locked all the doors. What we had overlooked
was that the French doors in the main room in Suriname only
locked from the inside. What could have been easier then, for an
ingenious packer than to leave the door unlocked, extract the music system from its box, hide it outside in a bush and come back for
it later? Suriname wins again.

From a letter to a friend – May 1998:

> We are now almost installed in a lovely elegant old house in
> a fine residential area near the centre of Port of Spain, a bus-
> tling and thriving city. It is a very different experience from
> Paramaribo's dilapidation and potholed roads. Port of Spain
> boasts whole strings of competing modern supermarkets, not to
> mention the shopping malls, art galleries and a couple of concert
> halls. We may miss the Bami and Nasi Goreng, and the jack-
> fruit sold off pickup trucks in the street, but we have plenty of
> local colour. Here we have the vendors of coconut water selling
> from fancy painted trucks around the fifteen-hectare Savannah,
> they decapitate the fresh coconuts with a lethal-looking cutlass
> in swashbuckling style and hand them over to be drunk through
> a straw. Fresh oysters are sold in the streets, and 'doubles' – a

pancake parcel wrapped around curried chickpeas – is widely eaten for breakfast, and lunch, and any time in between. 'Trinis' – as they love to be called – are great snackers, and there are innumerable delicacies to try and some we'd rather not. On daily visits to Star, in Curepe, we enjoyed the relish of local workers as they stopped by the stalls to devour such delights as oysters and hot sauce, pigs' feet, 'chicken-foot-souse' and 'gizzard pies'. We are also great readers of signs – we particularly like the church near our house which belongs to the 'Holy Confederation of Shouters' and we are rendered thoughtful by the many placards openly advertising in broad daylight: 'Foreign Body Parts for sale.' [Fortunately for cars, we later discovered.] The language too is a pleasure. We were initially delighted to be coming to an English-speaking culture again and it is certainly a plus to be able to answer the phone without breaking into a cold sweat about the rapid Dutch language at the other end of the line. Nevertheless, when two Trinidadians have a conversation in fast 'Trini' we realise that we have a lot to learn. The natural poetry of the language is a delight. Here, people don't take their passport or handbag to the airport, they: 'Walk wid de passport.' And you don't give a friend a lift in the car, you 'carry them' as in: 'I carryin' my mother to de hospital!' People don't 'see' something, they 'observe'; and they don't get angry – instead they 'vex big'. At the beginning of the rainy season a newspaper published pictures of some happy drenched folk with the caption: 'We's not afraid of de rain, we walk wit de raincoats.' A recent front-page scandal about an unfortunate gentleman who met an unfortunate end in a local hospital carried the headline: 'Who Pulled the Plug on Uncle Joe?' The very popular Catholic archbishop, Archbishop Anthon Pantin, was reproaching his congregation the other day for singing the national anthem with insufficient gusto, and came out with the immortal phrase: 'This is WE song!' And in a recent TV broadcast on the subject of Aids, the director of health concluded his speech with: 'For those of a mathematical disposition, the problem has increased exponentially. For those of you who are not, he gone up plenty!' And all of these beguiling expressions are delivered in the Trinidadian accent, with an intonation that sounds as if the speaker has just arrived from south Wales.

A few days after arriving, there was a ring at the gate. It was a representative of the Trinidad and Tobago water authority, armed with a form instructing him to turn off the water at the mains, since the bills had not been paid. I phoned the office. They checked. Yes it was true. Somehow, since the last delegate left a month ago it had been overlooked. Theresa, the office administrator was profuse in her apologies. Someone would go 'downtown' to pay it immediately. I relayed this to the overalled gentleman who was standing by the water mains, spanner at the ready. Could he PLEASE not turn the water off? It was being attended to. This was my second encounter with the Trinidadian love for rules and regulations.

'It sayin' here I have to turn de water off!' he said, flourishing his piece of paper.

No matter what I said, he insisted.

'Quod scripsi, scripsi!' It was written, and that was that.

The reply came back, like a refrain, 'I have to turn off de water.'

Finally I hit on a solution. 'OK,' I said. 'Turn the water off if you must, but then I want you to sit down there by the water mains, and wait. I'll bring you a cup of tea. When the bill is paid the office will phone and if you want you can speak to them. They will give you the numbers on the receipt and you can turn the water back on.'

And that is what we did. We waited solemnly for fifteen minutes, with the water turned off. He drank his tea. Then, when the moment came, it was firmly and legally turned back on again. We parted friends. And we had thought life in the Caribbean would be laid-back and devil-may-care!

We had arrived at the end of April. Europe Day is always held on 9th May. Could we possibly be ready in time? The house would have to be tidy – or packing cases hidden at least – and we would need to be on parade, looking relatively groomed, and ready to meet half of Trinidad. Invited guests would also have to be fed with canapés and snacks. Our efficient office administrator recommended a catering firm who could help.

The gate bell rang and two smiling ladies were at the door. They were attractive, warm, comfortable, and open, and they were wearing small crosses around their necks. I was about to encounter one of the most extraordinary groups of people I would ever meet, and certainly the most unusual catering firm. Sandra and Suzanne introduced themselves as the representatives of the 'Living Water Community'. They had come to talk about catering for Europe Day, to settle numbers and choose the snacks to be provided. They gave every impression of complete professionalism in what they did. When the business was over and the folder closed I had to ask them about themselves. What in the world was a religious community called 'Living Water' doing in the catering business? They invited me to come and see. And so, a few days later, I was at the door of the Living Water headquarters in Frederick Street 'downtown' ready to be shown around.

Living Water began in Port of Spain, in 1975, the vision of two women, Rhonda Maingot and Rose Jackman. Rhonda was a businesswoman and Rose an enclosed Dominican nun. They had never met but through a series of extraordinary events, each had simultaneously the same spiritual vision of starting a community to serve the people of Trinidad. And serve them they did. Starting small, they had evolved into a core community of twenty fully-committed people, lay men and women, and priests who lived in shared accommodation, prayed together, and were supported by an associate community of over five hundred covenanted members throughout Trinidad. Their main intention was to build a 'Civilisation of Love' in their care for their less fortunate brothers and sisters.

In rapid succession I was taken to see the huge, shining professional kitchen, the dining room where two to three hundred street people were given food at midday every day, the hospice, a house filled with mismatched rugs and curtains, and shining with joy, the home for babies with Aids, the project where unskilled girls were trained at long cutting tables to be highly skilled tailors in the fashion industry, the radio station, the chapel, the coffee shop and bookshop. I heard about the drugs rehabilitation work, the youth work, and the outreach to other countries in times of hardship or hurricane. The street people of Trinidad were especially cared for.

If an unfortunate soul was found lying in the gutter with people walking by, the police automatically called Living Water for help. It was the story of the Good Samaritan all over again. Even more remarkably, the group did all of its own fundraising via its 'other kitchen' – the cordon bleu kitchen where they could cater for up to two thousand for embassies, banks and big business, charging realistic prices for superb food. This was Robin Hood benevolence on a new scale, where the rich gladly paid for the welfare of the poor. I was shown round by a member of the community, a serene and enthusiastic Indian lawyer who had been convicted of fraud, and imprisoned. He had served his term and regarded his imprisonment and his subsequent life changes as the best thing that had ever happened to him.

When 'the girls' came to work at the house it was like having a group of friends to help. For Europe Day and all the functions that followed, they would turn up in good time in their van, dressed neatly in black trousers and white smocks and wearing simple crosses. Sometimes Sandra or Suzanne ran in ahead of time with a taste of some new recipe they had discovered. They brought with them their multiple trays of food and their portable oven. A list of vital timings would be pinned to a cupboard and they would set to work. I had the strongest impression that, if the ladies of Living Water were coming, even rain clouds would clear away. They cooked with Divine Intervention; I knew this for sure, because one evening as I went into the kitchen the soup was in trouble. Sandra was standing over the stove proclaiming in a loud voice: 'Oh Lord, help this soup!'

Europe Day that year was a resounding success, with the help of Living Water and the office staff. As usual, on these occasions, dressed in our best suits, we stood as a line of two hundred or so people filed in the front gate, shaking hands with all of them as we were introduced. KJ's second in command whispered information about them as they approached. As two rather large gentlemen approached, I remember him saying, very sotto voce 'Here come Tweedledum and Tweedledee!' but I have no idea why.

We were praying that we might remember at least a few names for the next hour or so. A steel pan band was playing softly at the gate. The illuminated blue and yellow flag was fluttering over the balcony. The night was balmy. Standing to one side and slightly to the back of the dais, I listened as KJ made a new Trinidadian version of his speech about the origins of the EU and its aims – not only in Europe, but in associated countries and, through emergency aid, throughout the world. He spoke sincerely. The speech was applauded. So was the fact that we were there, smiling and apparently fully organised at a major function, less than two weeks after arrival. A smiling Prime Minister Panday and his wife came. As I escorted Mrs Panday back down the drive to their car she took my hand and skipped along. Trinidad was certainly different.

'We couldn't have done this seven years ago when we started in Angola,' I thought, 'or at least not without nervous collapse.' Finally, the job was beginning to flow.

Among the guests at that first cocktail party were our next-door neighbours. We were living in St Clair, overlooking the Wildflower Park. No one seemed to know why it was called that since there was never a wildflower to be seen. Apart from the Japanese embassy on one side, and the Nigerian embassy across the road, we were almost surrounded by Sabgas. The Sabga clan was one of the numerous Lebanese families who prospered in Trinidad. They made up almost one per cent of the population. The brothers Ramon, Carlos and Richard Sabga were our neighbours. Their grandfather, Joseph, had arrived on the island in 1909 and had begun his commercial life peddling holy pictures from a portable barrow while waiting for the next boat to America. He fell in love with Trinidad and never caught that boat. Now, after generations of hard work, three grandsons were at the head of textile and property empires. Joseph had founded a dynasty. We met them on the Sunday after Europe Day. We were at the 'Vie de France' coffee shop in Maraval. A group of prosperous Middle Eastern businessmen were deep in conversation over breakfast at the next table obviously concluding deals, we thought. As we finished our coffee and croissants, one of them got up and came over to us.

'I'm your neighbour,' he said. 'I was at your house two nights ago.' Ignoring our embarrassment at not having recognised him from among two hundred guests, he said: 'Come and have some coffee, next door, about eleven o'clock.'

Despite being rather full of coffee just then, we agreed. It sounded like a royal summons, not to be refused. At 11 we presented ourselves at the big double gates next door. They swung silently open and we came into the grounds of a large modern two-storey white house. We were led through rooms of silk curtains, curvaceous, carved antique furniture, and tasteful silk flowers. On the patio were waiting Ramon, our host, and his dark-eyed wife Marie, his brother Richard and pretty wife Yvette, and brother Carlos. Polite and attractive teenage children made their appearance too. Sitting in straight-backed dignity was the matriarch, Mrs Charlotte Sabga. She ruled with benevolent dictatorship and knocked the brothers' heads together should they so far forget themselves as to quarrel. She was equal to any occasion, and had been known to send armed burglars running from her property by shouting at them as she would her children, from the top of the stairs: 'What's the matter with you? You crazy or something?'

A tray of Arabica coffee was brought and served, hot and bitter in fine china. There was an atmosphere of confident bonhomie. We felt that we were involved in a ceremony of introduction without necessarily knowing all the rubrics. I'm not sure that we ever did. The finer points of Arabic hospitality were never spelled out, but the welcoming generosity of our neighbours was unquestionable. Having made friends, there was warmth and advice ready to hand on any practical problem. Ramon's plumber and car mechanic were at our disposal. His electrician managed to bring half the municipal equipment to the door to change an electricity pole when we had a power 'outage'. Marie and I became firm friends and I spent many mornings perched on a stool in her huge kitchen, learning to make Lebanese dishes, then eating them together. I was shown shops and markets, the fish sellers on Carenage, nurseries and flower sellers. Often there would be a phone call in the early evening to say: 'I've just made kibbe! I'm coming to the fence with a plate for your supper.' And minutes later her smiling face would appear at the fence and plate of hot kibbe would he handed over, impeccably folded into silver foil.

Lebanese weddings were a revelation, filled with slim, glamorous young women in silver or gold lamé evening dresses, twirling to Arabic music. A Lebanese funeral could fill the largest church in Port of Spain with the descendants of the deceased unto the third and fourth generation. Many Lebanese wives in Trinidad had come from Lebanon as teenage brides. The ladies were beautifully groomed and ran their houses and families with utter confidence – not mere housewives but super-efficient domestic executives. Their children seemed to have escaped the ills of modern youth rebellion. Problems with drink or drugs seemed to be unknown, and the ease and social charm of the young people were remarkable. Devoutly Christian though these families were, we felt we had stepped back into an Old Testament biblical family structure – and one that seemed to work. And even more curiously, the warmth of family welcome with which we were surrounded was reminiscent of our Jewish family in Johannesburg, the Steiners, with whom we had spent many family Shabbat meals.

Our other next-door neighbour was the Japanese ambassador. His wife was a potter of professional standard, and entertained her guests with demonstrations of the tea ceremony, and recitals on the koto. Her dinner parties were legendary. With the help of the cooks provided to embassies by the Japanese Foreign Service, Japanese culture was represented most worthily. An invitation to a function was not to be missed, and dinner there was an assembly line of aesthetic experiences. The many courses were brought on exquisite lacquered services, each tiny morsel an adventure that lingered on the tongue – and all, of course, washed down with frequent toasts in sake or rice wine.

Misaki, talented though she was in so many respects, had one lacuna in her accomplishments. Her English was not good. However, she was under the delusion that she spoke English very well indeed, and forged ahead in conversation with reckless confidence. The only problem was that most of the time, what she said was almost completely incomprehensible. I can only conclude that she must have learned from a Japanese speaker with a very heavy accent. The crunch came one evening at a function held by the Ministry of Foreign Affairs. The headquarters were in one of the splendid old mansions around the Savannah. It was a recently refurbished wooden building, with brightly polished wooden floors. There were at least two hundred people present, all talking loudly in the echoing acoustics, and to make it worse, a steel band was playing on an open veranda nearby. Misaki approached purposefully in the midst of this din. I became aware that she was carrying on a conversation with me when I saw her lips moving. She might well have been saying something important. All I could hear were sounds like the occasional high-pitched squeaks of a bat being emitted at about the level of my bra. I tried desperately to look intelligent, and understanding, and nodded often and brightly, alternating my facial expressions between alert interest and intense concern, hoping one of these would be appropriate. She finally looked satisfied and moved away. Whatever had I missed – or agreed to – I will never know.

KJ too had his embarrassing moment with the representative of Japan although it is a moot point which of them was the more embarrassed. A new Japanese ambassador had arrived but we hadn't met him yet. The first opportunity came on the evening of the 'President's Award Ceremony' when prominent and high achieving citizens of Trinidad and Tobago were honoured. We noticed an unknown gentleman of oriental appearance arriving. KJ bounded over to be friendly, with his hand outstretched. The reaction was surprising. The new Japanese ambassador looked taken aback. He bobbed up and down in a random sort of way, in a state of extreme embarrassment. It was only when KJ got back to his seat that he realised what he had done. Ignorant of the finer points of Japanese courtesy he had neglected to offer a card. The poor ambassador had no idea who was addressing him, and therefore what degree of respect was due and how low to bow. KJ's good-natured gesture had thrown him into complete disarray.

While all of this was going on Star remained in quarantine. I negotiated the Lady Young mountain road every afternoon. Armed with a special permit to use the bus and taxi route, avoiding the rush-hour traffic, I dodged among the Maxi Taxis en route to Curepe, laden with comforts and treats of various kinds. I would then spend two hours sitting on the smelly concrete, hugging him, talking and inventing games. After the first few days he was cheerful, and even managed a few tiny welcome circles restricted by his tiny concrete kennel. We made friends with the kennel staff who, despite looking like ferocious Rasta pirates, were kindly men who did their best for the animals. They liked Star and would let him run up and down while they prepared the food.

We also made friends with a little cat, a thin, half-grown white kitten. Boasting an immense spiky tail like a bottlebrush, we nicknamed him 'Squirrel'. Squirrel had taken up residence at the kennels from who knows where, lured by the smell of dog food. We began to bring tins of cat food for him, and he would streak across the grass as soon as we arrived, emitting one unending, deafening meow that lasted the length of the property as he came, squirrel-tail held high in greeting. Very soon I could pick him up. One day one of the men at the kennels whispered that Squirrel was under a death sentence. The vet had said he must be put down, because stray animals could not wander around a quarantine kennel. This was a joke, since we could have brought any kind of infection in every day on our shoes but Squirrel, being cheeky, was walking on top of the wire cages, making faces at the dogs and driving them mad. There was only one thing to do. I bought a cat carrier, and, on the next visit, lured him in with mince and transported him home. We had acquired a cat.

At about the same time I looked out of a window one Saturday morning and saw a dog in the Wildflower Park. This was not too unusual. There were many stray dogs in Trinidad – too many. But this dog was walking in a strange, limping, hunched-up way, and finally lay down in a hollow under a tree. It was in trouble. Taking a piece of ham from the fridge and a blanket, we went over to investigate. KJ was wary. There was no need. It was a small black dog with brown Doberman eyebrows and no threat to anyone. Gentle by nature, she was so starved and ill-treated she could hardly move. We wrapped her in a rug and brought her back to the house. She had a tight string around her neck, and rope-burn marks on her chest and between the legs from the struggle for freedom. One back leg appeared to have been broken at some time. We took her to the nearest vet. Mitzi, as we christened her, came to live with us. She had a bed in the kitchen. Eventually her leg recovered and she began to put weight on it again. She was the gentlest soul but her reactions told us a story. Builders or anyone in overalls were bad news, as were ladders, or anyone carrying a bucket or a paint pot. Strange men walking too fast towards her reduced her into a cowering panic. Had she been tied up on a building site and mal-treated? She seemed to say so.

We were finding our way around Port of Spain. The trick to re-member was that everything goes around the Savannah in a clock-wise direction. Like a fifteen-hectare roundabout, it allowed cars to keep going around until they found the street they wanted. Or, if the turning was missed, go round again. The driving was inter-esting, in a dramatic and unexpected sort of way, but once in the stream of traffic, not as terrifying as it might have been. The style leaned towards spontaneity and liberation, as in: 'If ah in de left-hand lane and ah feel to turn right then ah do it, boy!'

Maxi Taxis were lethal, but confined to their own routes. Me-tered taxis, mostly very battered old Chevrolets, were not, and would cruise slowly around the Savannah in the left-hand lane, prepared to stop at a second's notice at the mere possibility of a fare. Travelling behind them was a collision waiting to happen.

KJ felt there was one crazy driver in every twenty – I rarely met them – but the rest seemed tolerant of each other's peccadilloes, and ours too which was just as well. Eye contact was useful. To get into a lane of traffic, a wound-down window and a pleading smile worked wonders, and having been let in, one then felt kindly disposed towards the next motorist stuck in the wrong lane. Traffic lights could be interesting. There was a local saying: 'Three on the yellow and two on the red!' – so it was a good idea to wait for them to come through after the light changed. And best not to stop too suddenly at a red light either, since the car behind wouldn't be expecting it. The cars on the road were a mixture of the new and the old. The 'Foreign Body Parts' advertised fitted the thousands of second-hand vehicles imported from America and Japan. But there were also cars that might have been on the road since the island's foundation, ancient sedans and utility trucks that were dented, rusted and battered, with stuffing coming out of the seats and no glass in the windows. Friends of ours had one that needed to be started with a dessertspoon instead of a key.

I joined a gym. To get there involved driving around the Savannah. The gyms all opened at 4.30 a.m. to beat the heat. I would leave the house at 5, in the dark. By 5.15 a.m. the paved track around the edge of the park was teeming with people in the half-light, some walking, some running, some already finished their exercise for the day and doing their stretches on the benches. I amused myself counting the numbers. On a slow morning there might be ninety keen exercisers, and on a busy one, anything up to a hundred and fifty. This increased mightily after Christmas, we heard, when everyone woke up to the fact that they had to fit a great deal of Christmas dinner into an extremely small sparkling bikini by Carnival time.

The gym itself was unlike any other I had belonged to. The manager and chief trainer was Colin Seabright, a bodybuilder and gentle giant over six feet tall and, it seemed, at least four feet wide at the shoulders. He looked stunning in his gym clothes, but any suit he wore looked several sizes too small and his Mr Universe physique immediately turned him into Michelin man. 'Going to de gym' was a joyous occasion, as were most things in Trinidad. Music played constantly – lively Caribbean music, and people danced from one machine to the other. The highly efficient trainers jived too, and laughed and chatted with the members while keeping an eye on our performance. Coffee and cakes were available in the foyer and Colin organised bicycle rides at weekends to offset the cakes. Walking on the treadmill was not the boring experience it is in Europe. Plate glass windows looked out over the Savannah. There was an unending procession of passersby to watch in the brilliant sunshine. People were running and walking with dogs, ladies walking with their prams, old couples taking sedate exercise, fruit sellers in headscarves, athletes with honed muscles doing serious training – and once a Rasta running with dreadlocks so long that his heels kicked them up at every step.

Trinidadians are early risers and late revellers. In fact no one knew when they slept. Parties, restaurants, fetes, dancing, and concerts went on until the small hours, steel bands rehearsed all night, the exercising started before dawn and offices opened at 7.30. A Trinidadian friend, a busy interior designer, complained that she would soon have to be up at 3 a.m. to do her housework, her yoga, her meditation and her exercise before work. No wonder everyone was hungry and streaming out to snack bars by 11 a.m. for roti or doubles. Or did they all just fall asleep at their desks?

By KJ's account, they did not. These friendly, smiling people of the rainbow nation epitomised the joyous, laid-back Caribbean nature with their calypsos, their steel pan, and their soca music, their rum punch and their Carnival. But play was play and work was work. In the office, procedures, hierarchy and rules abounded. We had discovered this when we tried to circumvent the rules for Star, and when the water engineer simply had to turn off the water because it said so on a piece of paper. In the workplace people dressed formally in smart business suits, and took life seriously. Documents and papers passed from desk to desk, referred upwards ad infinitum in due order awaiting the stamp of someone with sufficient authority to make a final decision. Some small irregularity could cause months, or even years, of delay.

A case in point was the story of the Six Suitcases. KJ had a Technical Assistant who had come to Trinidad to work on an agricultural project. He was a bachelor, and did not bring much with him. For some reason however, his goods – six suitcases – were immediately impounded in customs.

Phone calls were made but nothing happened. A meeting was called. When KJ arrived the Minister of Agriculture was there, plus two lawyers and a customs official. The matter was brought up. Notes were made. The minister assured KJ that it would be dealt with. And nothing happened.

More phone calls were made at regular intervals. Nothing happened.

It was then said to be a more serious matter that had passed to the legal department. A meeting was held at the Attorney General's office. The Attorney General, his Permanent Secretary, and the Permanent Secretary of Agriculture were there plus lawyers and two representatives from customs – all for six suitcases. The Attorney General upbraided people and made assurances that it would be sorted out. Nothing happened.

Despite all the meetings and VIPs present the poor man's suitcases remained firmly locked away. Finally they were released six months later, in time for the owner's departure. Perhaps the equivalent of Star's C63 form had not been correctly filled in. No one ever knew.

Was this unexpected legalism a result of overzealous training during British colonial days? Or could there have been something even deeper, reaching back into the days of slavery and ingrained in the very DNA, some deep damage stemming from a time when decisions were the province of the Master, and only those in the highest authority could have the final word? When making a mistake or an assertion could be followed by severe punishment or death and the only safety the law. In the Caribbean, 99.9% of the Afro-Caribbean population is there because of some connection with slavery. We of European origin need to remember this often with shame and compassion. History, combined with the pronounced Caribbean distaste for being wrong, which seemed more than the normal human reaction, made us resolve to be sensitive and observant in our dealings with Trinidadian friends.

7

Trinidad: A Carnival of Cultures

Who were our Trinidadian friends? Outgoing and warm, party-loving and generous, Trinidadians took us to their hearts. I had the impression that, as a European, one was weighed up in an instant. If I smiled at the checkout girl at the supermarket with openness and warmth, after a moment of doubt, that smile would come back magnified. Fruit sellers and florists, booksellers and fishermen all responded to us like long lost friends. Hugs and greetings were everywhere. I was told that Trinidadians found KJ and me 'endearing' although we never quite knew exactly what that meant. But as we all do, Trinis loved their country to be appreciated.

Soon after we arrived the festival of Hosay took place. Huge, colourful papier-mâché models of the world's great mosques were built by the Muslim population of Port of Spain, and paraded through the streets with drumming and dancing. I was standing on the balcony of the house, jumping up and down and enjoying the procession as it passed, clapping my hands and stomping my feet in time to the drums. Earl, KJ's driver, arrived and caught me at it. I was embarrassed. He looked approving, and said: 'You were really grooving!'

For once I understood what Earl had said. He was one of the friendliest and most helpful people anyone could meet, with a ready smile and an infectious laugh, but he was also quite possibly the fastest speaker in Port of Spain, if not the whole of Trinidad and Tobago, particularly when in full flow with a friend. In those early days I usually knew what he meant, but rarely knew exactly what he had said.

Hosay was our first introduction to the procession of festivals that stud the year in Trinidad and Tobago. The list of public holidays was a calendar of cross-cultural history.

On New Year's Day, everyone was recovering from all the 'Old Year's Night' parties and the fireworks on the Savannah. In March, the Spiritual Shouter Baptist Liberation Day was the newest public holiday and was marked by religious rallies. In April on Good Friday, a large percentage of Trinidad went to church and ate 'provisions', mountainous plates of dry multicoloured sweet potatoes. They made an appropriately penitential lunch, and brought back memories of Africa and the diet of slave times. Easter Monday was a day for visiting, and going to the races in Arima. On 30th May was Indian Arrival Day and its street procession of floats depicted the arrival of indentured labourers from India. June brought Corpus Christi, and the Labour Day procession. The first of August was Emancipation Day, a lively procession celebrating the end of slavery in Trinidad. Everyone wore brilliantly coloured African costumes, and rejoiced. The thirty-first of August was Independence Day, 24th September brought Republic Day and in October the festival of Eid ul Fitr was celebrated by the Muslim community who shared sweetmeats with all their friends. In November everyone celebrated Diwali with the Hindu population. Diwali lights and Indian sweetmeats were handed out at the supermarket checkouts. Spicy food was served on banana leaves. Twinkling lights decorated the St James area of Port of Spain and houses belonging to East Indian families were outlined with lights and little candles. An evening drive 'to South' was a twinkling fairyland of delight – clay deya lights lined paths and garden beds and the roofs and eaves of the houses dripped white light icicles.

After Diwali, everyone, including the Indian population, put up their Christmas trees and the town went crazy for Christmas lights, and shopping. 'Downtown' was a riot of red and green, glitter and tinsel, and street traders thronged the kerb. Christmas meant new clothes for everyone and the textile emporiums which ran the length of Frederick Street had standing room only as a heaving mass of enthusiastic humanity shopped for brightly coloured Christmas materials, dress and curtain fabrics. This was another relic of slave times, when cloth for new garments was given at Christmas. Now Trinis like to have new curtains and new upholstery in the house as well, and cast-offs are passed on to less fortunate families.

'Parang' groups do the rounds of parties singing lively Venezuelan Christmas songs in Spanish to the accompaniment of guitar, cuatro, mandolin and tea-chest bass. There is much visiting and much consumption of the sweet red sorrel drink, and 'ponche crème' – a potent rum, cream and sugar concoction containing at least a million calories per glass. And of course, whereas in other countries there is a lull after Christmas, and spirits fall, in Trinidad there is Chinese New Year to look forward to, with more fireworks and then, finally, the mother and father of all festivals at the beginning of Lent: CARNIVAL.

The joy of it all was that in this multiracial, multicultural nation, everybody celebrated everything. Whereas in Suriname people were aware of each other's festivals, in Trinidad everyone got involved. We all loved and lit Diwali lights, we all turned out for the processions and most people celebrated Christmas in some form or other. We were beginning to sense that there was no way of understanding the cross-currents and rip tides of this multi-ethnic society without understanding something of its history.

Who were the Trinidadians and how did they come to be there?

As in Suriname, agricultural Amerindian tribes were followed by the Arawak hunters, and their enemies the Caribs who slowly spread through the islands, and gave the region its name. Now the only organised group of Amerindian descent in Trinidad is the Santa Rosa Carib community in the town of Arima. Our dear housekeeper Beverley bore her Amerindian ancestry with pride. Names such as Curepe, the Ariapita and Mucurapo business streets in town, and Tunapuna on the outskirts of Port of Spain remain on the map to remind present-day Trinidad of its early inhabitants.

Into this region of forest-dwellers came the Spanish. Christopher Columbus 'discovered' the island of Trinidad by accident in July 1498. One of his sailors, Alonzo Perez Nirando, spotted an island with three mountains. He named it 'Trinidad' – the island of the Trinity. And thinking that they had arrived in India the inhabitants were called 'Indians' – later modified to 'West Indians' – European explorers never liked to be proved wrong.

The island remained in Spanish hands for the next three centuries. Since the dream of Spanish explorers was 'Eldorado', interest faded when no 'man of gold' was found and no rich gold mines. The Amerindian population dwindled, wiped out by European diseases, and cruelty. Unwilling slaves, the Amerindians wanted as most of us do to live their own lives in peace. They resisted efforts at enslavement, constantly ran away to regain their freedom, and were cruelly punished with ingenious tortures for their perceived 'misdeeds'.

In 1783 French settlers arrived. They were tempted to come by a Spanish decree which offered free land grants to Roman Catholic settlers of 'any friendly nation' (i.e. anyone but the British). Settlers were granted thirty-two acres per person if they were white-skinned and sixteen acres if they were 'Free persons of Colour'. Both groups were entitled to eight acres for every slave they brought with them. Not surprisingly, everyone arrived with as many slaves as they could afford, and there was a sudden increase in the population. In that era of tumultuous and bloody revolutions, French-speaking people, both royalists and republicans, were attracted to the safety of Trinidad, and flocked in from Haiti and other French-speaking Caribbean islands. Today in Trinidad noble French names like de l'isle, de Verteuil, and de la Motte are borne by people in all walks of life, from government ministers to the fruit seller at the corner.

This edict was the real beginning of large-scale slavery in Trinidad. With it the plantation economy was truly born. Cotton, sugar, coffee and cocoa plantations boomed. At the same time as the European and African population soared, the original population of forty thousand Amerindians was reduced to only 1127. There were two unusual factors in Trinidad – none of the slaves had come directly from Africa, all were second or third generation slaves, mostly from other Caribbean islands. They were 'seasoned' as it was then called, meaning that their spirit was broken and they were less likely to rebel. In addition there was a large 'Free Coloured' slave-owning class, highly educated migrants from other Caribbean islands.

And then in 1797, the British attacked. Greatly outnumbered, the Spanish governor decided to capitulate, with a grand gesture. Before handing over the island to the British invaders Chacon gave orders that all the Spanish ships in Chaguaramas Bay were to be burnt. The British gained a colony but had to stand by and watch the conflagration of the Spanish ships which could have served them well. For the next one hundred and sixty-five years Trinidad would remain a British colony with a twist. Ruled by a British governor it would nevertheless operate in French retaining a largely French-speaking population, but ruled by a Spanish legal code.

The British General Picton was appointed Military Governor. Aware of the revolutionary goings-on in France, he viewed all French Creoles, particularly republicans, with suspicion and distaste. He wanted no such trouble in his colony. On the slightest pretext, anyone suspected of republicanism was sent to the gallows or tortured. Hundreds fled. The tensions that arose then between French and English can still be sensed today.

Ten years after the British takeover, in 1807, the Slave Trade was abolished although full emancipation only came in 1834. Slave numbers were small in Trinidad in comparison to islands like Haiti where slavery was on an industrial scale and slaves were worked to death. But now the composition of the Trinidadian slave population changed. Under the British, slaves had been brought in direct from Africa – from Nigeria, Ghana and the Congo. Recently arrived, 'unseasoned' and still retaining their sense of dignity, their language and culture, these new slaves were not cowed, and would put a strong stamp on the emerging society of Trinidad – to this day remarkable for its energy, fire and self-esteem. Among them was a Muslim group called the Mandingoes from West Africa. One of them, a dignified freed slave called Johannes Mohammed Bath bought the freedom of other Muslim slaves from Senegambia as they arrived. He would go to the port as the slave ships arrived and address the new arrivals with a 'Salaam'. Those who answered with 'Salaam Alaikum' would be bought by him and would become part of his Islamic group. They in time became powerful property owners and evolved into the present-day Islamic organisation in Trinidad: Jamaat al Muslimeen.

But now the international slave trade had ended. No new slaves would arrive. The planters were desperate. They had huge plantations but no future workforce. It was therefore decreed that their present slaves – who should by now have been free men – must continue working for their masters for another six years as 'apprentices'. Understandably the slaves saw through the ploy and protested. A crowd gathered at government house shouting: 'Pas de six ans, point de six ans!'

Efforts were made to bring labour from the US, Europe, Madeira and China. Then indentured Indian labourers were sought. Up to 1917 over one hundred and forty thousand people were brought to the island from India. The arrival and details of every Indian worker is minutely recorded in ledgers in the Public Records Office, and Indian Arrival Day is celebrated every year. Although the Indian workers were theoretically 'indentured' for five years, they might as well have been slaves. Their hours of work in the cane fields were back-breaking and, at any one time, hundreds were in jail for breaking the terms of their contract. They were free to return to India at the end of their contract but many preferred to take up smallholdings of land or start small businesses. Today in Trinidad, political power is split almost equally between Afro- and Indo-Trinidadian descendants of workers imported by the one-time colonial masters.

The 'Rainbow Nation' of Trinidad is a true melting pot. Trinidadians like to call it a 'Callaloo', after their favourite soup – a mixture of many ingredients. There are people of Spanish, French, British and Portuguese descent, West Africans from Ghana, Nigeria, Senegal and Gambia, there are the descendants of Chinese Haka people, East Indian people Shi'ite Muslims, Syrians and Lebanese and the strong and beautiful mixture that is Caribbean Creole. Is it any wonder it was so colourful and exciting to live there? I would walk down the street feeling a sense of home. In such a multicoloured society, everyone was acceptable, even a conspicuously blonde Australian.

The one event that brings all of Trinidad together is Carnival. It is held, according to tradition, on the three days leading to Ash Wednesday every year. Only Rio's carnival is larger. It begins with Jouvay – 'Jeu Ouvert' – at midnight on Carnival Monday, when bands of revellers go out, dressed in coloured rags, portraying sinister devils or blue 'jab jab' men, bats and 'midnight robbers'. The bands dance around the town, singing, playing loud music, rolling barrels of beer, and taking every opportunity to throw mud and coloured paint at each other until dawn. At dawn the revellers go home, shower off the mud and dirt of the previous year, and with the rising sun, come out in the gold and silver and spangles of Carnival proper. They put on their 'Pretty Mas' – the Pretty Masquerade costumes they have saved for all year – and go out into the streets.

Carnival is three days of dancing, drinking singing fun, open to everyone. All of the cultural groups pool their talents, forging a unique event. Out of the diversity, something new is created. It is a gigantic safety-valve, releasing a whole year's worth of tensions. Not only do people sing and dance out their frustrations, but the calypso tradition gives cheeky calypsonians the freedom to poke fun at all groups in 'no holds barred' social and political satire. Reminiscent of the biting satire of Alexander Pope, calypso helps people to laugh at themselves and their politicians instead of erupting in anger. Trinidadians are not noted for their reticence, but this is one time of the year when they have the freedom to express anything. Carnival nourishes the musical, artistic and cultural life of the island and, like a good school play – everyone gets involved. It is a cohesive force in the community. People are so busy enjoying themselves that crime is minimal. A pickpocket is likely to be chased and caught by the irate crowd and chastised for spoiling de fun. On one occasion a thief, having been caught, was stripped of his five pairs of multi-pocketed shorts, and the purse restored to its owner to the sound of cheering. More than a million people are on the streets in a spirit of pure enjoyment. When, after three days of non-stop dancing and fun, people creep home at dawn on Ash Wednesday to take off their by now bedraggled finery, the problems of a week ago no longer seem so important.

The whole history of Trinidad can be traced in Carnival. Each nation that came to Trinidad has left its mark. The Spanish held 'disguise balls' but it was not until the French came in the 1780s that the Mediterranean Mardi Gras and its carnival characters arrived. 'Dame Lorraine' with her satirically exaggerated crinoline, and traditional Pierrot costumes still appear. The first celebrations were held on the old sugar plantations. Whites would don fancy costume, aping the dress and activities of their slaves. They would dress as a 'negre jardim' or 'garden boy' in ragged breeches and a blackened face – that character's sequinned shirt, breeches and stick became an accepted carnival character. Ladies found it amusing to blacken their faces and dress as 'Mulatresses'. But it was not all one-sided. The African slaves observed the carryings-on – probably with some amusement – and in their compound, parallel festivities grew up, imitating and guying their masters. Whereas the white ladies blackened their faces the slaves whitened theirs with flour, saying: 'See we white face, we white wig!' A contemporary account, written by a European, says: 'Every Negro, male and female, wore a white flesh coloured mask, their woolly hair carefully concealed by handkerchiefs, this contrasted with the black bosom and arms was droll in the extreme!' No doubt the slaves thought their black-faced masters and mistresses looked just as ridiculous.

Camboulay – a corruption of 'Cannes Brûlées' (Burning Cane) evolved from the celebrations after a cane fire, when slaves would be called out with horns, conch shells and the cracking of whips to put out the blaze. Afterwards, there would be rejoicing, Kalenda or African stick fighting, music and dancing. Camboulay moved into the streets and became so wild and threatening that it was banned, which led to riots. Later it reappeared as the 'Jouvay' opening event of carnival Saturday – now the horns and conch shells are replaced by gigantic speakers on trucks, and are even noisier.

Ancient costumes can still be seen in modern Carnival, although in recent years sequinned bikinis and designer carnival bands predominate. But elements of the 'Old Mas' can be seen, echoing Trinidad society through the ages. There is the police and thief re-enactment – sometimes played out in reality. There are the

Congo bands – using drums and wearing costumes decorated with beads, feathers and jewelled anklets, led by gigantic Carnival kings and queens. There are the Moka Jumbies (stilt-walkers) coming from a West African depiction of a guardian spirit who is raised above mere mortals and can see trouble coming from his elevated position. There are fancy Indians, harking back to Amerindian ancestors, and fancy sailors, reflecting the days of sailing ships, and the highly suggestive, hip-rotating 'wining' carnival dance descends from 'jamette' – from the French word *diamètre*; activities from the fringes of society far outside the diameter of respectability.

In the *Port of Spain Gazette*, a nineteenth century 'Mr Disgusted' wrote: 'We will not say how many we saw in a state so nearly approaching nudity, as to outrage decency, and shock modesty… but we will say at once, that the custom of keeping Carnival, by allowing the lower order of society to run about the streets in wretched masquerade, belongs to other days, and ought to be abolished in our own.' What would he say today?

Carnival has become one of the world's biggest parties. It is a case of join in or leave Trinidad for the duration. At our first carnival we had no idea what to expect. There had been a whole year of preparation that we knew nothing about. Prior to the event there had been weeks of competitions, the Panorama Steel Pan Championships with bands from all over the world, the soca music competitions, and the road songs. In the calypso tents on the Savannah, calypsonians with names like 'The Mighty Sparrow', 'Lord Kitchener', 'Cro Cro' and 'Scrunter' competed until the small hours for their titles, singing songs of biting satire and social protest – all of them rendered in fluent Trini, at maxi decibels. I went with protective earplugs tucked into my handbag together with a fan. Sometimes still, on opening a handbag, I find these nostalgic objects lying at the bottom and the moist heat and the decibels rush back into awareness.

We went to the grandstand in the middle of the Savannah to see the kings and queens of Carnival parading in their massive twenty-foot-high and -wide costumes, 'worn' or semi-carried by strong, muscular men and women. The costumes, more like constructions, were executed by 'de wire benders' in wire and gauze, and millions of psychedelic sequins, and were so heavy and elaborate they needed wheels to help them roll across the stage. There were butterflies, flowers, and hummingbirds, representations of poetry, myth and legend. Venus the Queen of Love was there, and Mars the God of War in all his golden glory, whole ships and cities sailed across the stage and peacocks strutted with firecrackers in their tails.

On the night of Jouvay we were a little nervous. We didn't quite know what to do or what would happen. The sound of music with a loud beat was in the air as we sat in the garden. By the time we went to bed it was getting louder. By midnight the Jouvay processions, the devils and jab jab men were abroad, and the beat from dozens of ten-foot-high speakers was coming past our front gate. All the window frames of the old house rattled as the speaker trucks rolled past. Too timid to go out and join in, we retreated to a back room with earplugs, and slept on sun lounges, clutching Squirrel, the cat.

The next morning we opened our eyes into Trinidad's bright sunshine. But it was a different Trinidad. The light in the garden looked brighter, trees and flowers seemed to sparkle, the lawns looked greener and an excited electricity was buzzing in the air. Even the trees and flowers seemed to be spinning and vibrating with energy and excitement. After breakfast we went to explore. As Beverley had excitedly told us, the streets were full of happy people 'chipping along' with a little dislocated step and sway behind their favourite steel pan bands on 'de pan trucks'. Some were in costume, or partly so; some were already formed into small bands, a few of the smaller Carnival kings and queens were already on the street – but only those that could fit under the telegraph wires. Food sellers were doing a roaring trade and the air was full of the smell of hot roti and doubles. But that was only the beginning.

On Carnival Tuesday we had invitations to sit in the grandstand at the Savannah. The band of Peter Minshal would make its appearance. Peter was known as the 'Master of Mas'. He had designed for the opening of the Olympic Games in Los Angeles, Atlanta and

Barcelona. A theatrical genius trained at the Central School of Art and Design in London, he had raised Carnival to a high art form. He did not just design costumes for a band, he created an event; a poetic myth that did not merely parody local conditions, but forced the onlooker to reflect on ideas of earthly, even cosmic, significance. He spoke of 'guiding the collective soul into the brave new millennium'. 'Paradise Lost', 'Zodiac', 'Halleluiah', 'Danse Macabre', and 'Song of the Earth' were some of his past themes. One year he had created 'The Rat Race' – thousands of rats (mother rats, father rats, little rats, doctor rats, lawyer rats, noble rats, poor rats) with a satirical story to match. We would hear, when we came to know him, of his delight as a small boy when, dressed up as a 'Dame Lorraine' on Jouvay night, and wearing a stocking over his head, he found he had the power to embarrass a less than favourite teacher. Today he was bringing his band across the Savannah at noon. This year's myth concerned 'The Lost Tribe'. Trinidadians in their thousands, truly a new tribe from so many lands, swept across the Savannah in the full glare of the midday sun to the sound of Bedouin music, dressed in Arab costumes in earth colours.

For twelve hours, mile after mile of carnival procession paraded around the town and across the grass of the Savannah. Up to ten thousand people in each band danced, and wined their way around the town, the men dressed as plumed Inca warriors, Roman centurions, pirates and warriors (sometimes with boxer shorts for modesty). The ladies, regardless of their size, were resplendent in showgirl spangled bikinis, kicking up their legs, slim or ample – all wearing gold-dyed trainers for the survival of their feet. The music trucks interspersed the procession, playing the freshly composed road songs at deafening volume; after all, the song that was sung the most often would win a car. The chief contender that year seemed to be one with a very odd chorus. It sounded to us like 'ass in the air, ass in the air' – and looking at the high-kicking dancers it seemed feasible. Only later did we find out that it was 'ash in the air!' – though who knew why?

There were bands of the old characters, there were blue bands carrying moons and stars, green bands saluting nature, red bands of flames and demons, pink bands of fluffy pom-poms, silver bands clad in tinsel and gold bands waving smiling suns. There was a circus band with ringmaster and a full team of performers in animal costumes. But perhaps the most exciting band of all was called 'The River Nile'. Thousands of revellers danced and writhed past, in costumes depicting all of the countries through which the river flowed – led by the 'Queen of Sheba' on a golden throne, who was carried by a dozen 'Nubian slaves'; oiled muscle-men from the city gyms.

After watching for seven hours we went home and turned on the TV. It was still happening. Bands continued to parade ever more raggedly until nightfall. The streets were by now blowing with tired fragments of costume, and the whole event was coming apart at the seams. Not even 'Trinis' can dance non-stop for three days. Some of the Carnival kings and queens had collapsed, exhausted with the effort of dragging their gigantic costumes all day. There lay the costumes on the side of the road, gorgeously coloured mythical creatures, looking like dinosaurs that had been shot down, toppled to one side, and waiting to be helped home by friends.

At midnight, the entire populace turned back into rats and pumpkins. Cinderella went home, washed, changed and appeared in church on Ash Wednesday morning. Having demurely received ashes on her forehead she would be back in the kitchen, or at the office desk. By 9 a.m. the cast-off glass slippers, gold crowns, tridents and beer cans were already swept and tied up in hundreds of black dustbin bags all round the Savannah. Stray dogs were sniffing for bits of sausage and roti. The city was left with that sense of flat fizz that comes after a really great party. Tired revellers repaired to Maracas beach and Tobago to recover. After a sleep, committees would soon begin meeting again to design next year's costumes, and round about November every year there is always an unaccountable bulge in the birth rate.

Trinidad Callaloo Soup
(can add a pork rib or crabmeat)

About 12 dasheen leaves (or bhagi or large spinach)
2 cups coconut milk
1 tbsp butter
1 scotch bonnet pepper
8 ochroes
2 sprigs thyme
1 onion
4 chives
1 cup boiling water
1 small packet fish/vegetable stock cubes.

Strip the stalks and midrib from the dasheen or spinach
leaves and wash well. Wash and cut up the ochroes and
seasonings. Put all the ingredients, except the butter, into
a pot with the boiling water and simmer until everything
is soft (keep the hot pepper near the surface). Add 2 or 3
stock cubes and adjust to taste. Remove the pepper and
blend the ingredients into a puree. Add the butter.

8

Star and Other Creatures

We booked a trip to Grande Riviere, a beach on the north coast of Trinidad where giant leatherback turtles came to lay their eggs. It was recommended by Luigi, the Italian engineering advisor at the office, for its gourmet Italian food. We thought he should know.

We set off on the two hour drive, heading east from Port of Spain, past Piarco airport, and Arima, cutting through to the coast road via little beach towns with storybook names like Sangre Grande, Toco, Matelot and Sans Souci. As we went the winding road became narrower and riddled with potholes. Local pickup trucks shot around corners on the wrong side of the road – sometimes because their side of the road had disappeared, washed away and all but fallen into the sea. We passed a sad tethered donkey carrying a monstrous load of grass and a duck sitting in a tree. The mountain roads were thickly forested with big timber and tree ferns. Cliff-sides were thick with mosses and tree ferns that would cost a fortune at a London florist. Scarlet heliconias flashed in the undergrowth. Almost at the end of the line came Grande Riviere. As we approached the turning to the town, a grey horse ambled across the road. We stopped the car and he put his thoroughbred nose in the window. When we arrived at the Mon Plaisir Hotel we mentioned him with some anxiety.

'Oh that's all right,' said the receptionist in the dark concrete reception area. 'That Celebration Time, he walkin' up de village, but he comin' home nights.'

We hadn't known what to expect. Whatever we had had in mind it was not this. 'Mon Plaisir' was an old coffee plantation now restored by Piero Guerini, an Italian photojournalist who had fallen in love with it. The hotel was a series of basic low wooden buildings running along the beachfront. The cement floored dining area had wooden tables, driftwood decorations and home-made arches looking over the beach. Piero's retired racehorse, Celebration Time, would occasionally put his head through the arches for a pat, and to see what guests were having for breakfast. The rooms were small and painted in bright primitive murals, their stable doors opening directly on to the sand. Air conditioning was operated by opening a window. Mosquito nets were braided into round coronets and once released, cascaded down over the beds. Sleep came to the sound of breaking surf, every wave sounding a unique rhythmic pattern.

The Italian cuisine was happily married to local, freshly caught fish. We attended a talk about the UN project that had assisted in training local young men to guard and monitor the turtles. Instead of slaughtering them for meat as their forefathers might have done, these young lads woke willing visitors and carefully guided them to watch the turtles laying their hundreds of eggs, explaining the process with the least disturbance to the animals. In the morning any hatchlings would be gathered up before the packs of village dogs or the black Trinidadian vultures, the hunched 'Corbeaux' (Cobboes), could swoop. The babies would be kept moist in shallow water until nightfall, when they would be released at the water's edge. Under the shelter of night, a percentage might survive predators on their journey of many thousands of miles.

We had agreed to be woken for the Turtle Watch. At 11 p.m. there was muted excitement on the beach and torchlight in the distance. We stumbled in silence along the soft lumpy sand to where a giant turtle was preparing to lay her eggs. The size of an oval dining room table, the prehistoric amphibian lay on the sand, laboriously scooping out a hollow with her flippers. Once done, she began laying her soft round, dented eggs, each one the size of a golf ball. The process was long and tears streamed down her face as she lay there. Despite our compassionate fantasies, the tears were a protective response to flying sand. Once done, she began to cover up her nest. Round and round she went, covering her traces first in one direction and then another to confuse her enemies. The sand was a minefield of flipper tracks as she laboriously dragged her heavy body round in circles. Finally it was done. She rested with exhaustion. A few more turns and she was facing the sea. Moonlight shining on the waves drew her in the right direction. Slowly she dragged herself flipper by heavy flipper towards the edge of the water. As she rested there, the first waves washed over her. Dragged by the undertow, she began to budge. The next wave and then the next floated her. Suddenly, no longer a clumsy tank on land, she was swimming strongly, head held up in the moonlight until, with one last glimpse, she was on her way.

We fell into bed under the mosquito nets. But it was a short night. An hour or two later I was awakened by a knocking sound.

'Shh!' I hissed at KJ. The sound came again. I tried something louder. When the noise continued I said, 'Be quiet!'

A plaintive voice came from the other side of the room. 'But it's not me!'

We got up to investigate. Out on the beach a large turtle was knocking her shell against the corner of the hut, turning in slow desperate circles as she tried to find the sea. She had finished laying her eggs and had mistaken the hotel's security lighting for moonlight shining on the water. KJ found a solid piece of driftwood and as we had seen the guide do, we planted it in the sand on the landward side of the turtle. She was hard-wired to move away from obstacles – rather like a robotic vacuum cleaner. Every time her shell touched the wooden pole she moved away from it and in agonisingly slow dot and carry, we guided her away from the alien place of lights and human beings and towards the sea. Shepherding this lumbering prehistoric beast back to her own element, it was hard to imagine that she would be agile and graceful once in the water. Finally she reached the sea. She floated with the first wave, and drifted with the second, becoming light and agile, and with the third wave she was swimming. We watched, like proud parents, until she disappeared from sight.

The next morning Mon Plaisir had other surprises for us, quite apart from the freshly squeezed fruit juice and the stack of American-style pancakes. The turtle season had started early and there were already a few babies hatching out. Sitting in the open-air dining room KJ felt something crawling on his foot. Looking down we saw that baby turtles, too, could take the wrong direction. There was a hatchling, four inches long, energetically hauling itself along on the concrete floor, making frantic non-stop swimming motions with its flippers like a battery-powered toy, in preparation for that grand moment when it would launched itself into the waves. Incredibly, these tiny mites will remember the beach where they hatched, and twenty-five years on, having circumnavigated the globe, will return to lay their own eggs, in the place where they themselves were born.

Back in the room there was a sound at the window. A green parrot with rings of rainbow feathers around its neck was perched on a branch, looking in, bright eyed. I put out my hand and he jumped on to it. The little feet were warm, not cold and scratchy as I had feared. Carefully bringing him back inside we made friends. He was happy to be petted and insisted on staying on my shoulder for the morning. Not a lover of men, he hissed when KJ came near. He and his brother were pets. Some Trinidadians raise parrots by hand from the egg so that they are habituated to human company. These two liked people so much there was no need of restraint. They flew wild in the trees, and came to their perches when they felt like it. Their trust of people gave them the confidence to land unannounced on the shoulders of unsuspecting guests. It sometimes caused consternation and more than a few expletives.

We began to explore more of Trinidad. It is not a tourist island – Tobago is the palm-fringed paradise sown with hotels. Trinidad is the place where Trinis live and work. But there are treasures to be found.

The Asa Wright bird sanctuary is in the Northern Range above Arima. It was a two-hour drive from Port of Spain along hair-raising roads through old plantations of coffee and cocoa, all now overgrown with tall vegetation. Just before the bird sanctuary the country opened out. There before us was an entire hillside netted over. Interlaced vines grew on the netting with a gourd-like vegetable hanging from the nets like large green Christmas decorations.

The farm was surrounded by Hindu prayer flags, which added to the festive effect. It was a crop of 'christophine' a popular local vegetable, known elsewhere as chayote squash. Originally the 'Spring Hill Estate', the Asa Wright sanctuary had been a plantation too, for coffee, cocoa and citrus. Its two thousand acres stand twelve hundred feet above sea level, overlooking the Arima and Aripo valleys. We sat on the veranda of the old plantation house, our eyes glued to rows of bird feeders hanging along the eaves, as dozens of tiny hummingbirds hovered to take up the sweet liquid. We were on their level as they sipped, pale blue, lime green, turquoise, peacock-blue and purple, shimmering and quivering as their tiny humming wings supported them. In the shrubbery and on the ground were dozens – even hundreds – of small and larger birds. The names read like a bird-watcher's incantation:

White-bearded Manakin, and Violacious Trogon,
Topaz Hummingbird and Tufted Coquette,
White-necked Jacobin, Chestnut Woodpecker,
Channel–billed Toucan,
Blue-crowned mot-mot,
Bearded Bell-bird,
And Great Ant-Shrike…

Nearby Crested Oropendolas flew in and out of the larger trees, trees full of long pendulous nests like high-rise avian apartment blocks. Trapeze artists of the bird world, these large black birds with flashy yellow tails clung to the dangling nests, and opening their wings, they swung round in dizzy circles, uttering a cry that was a cross between musical gurgle and whistle. On the ground, a sleek auburn-coated agouti (a tailless squirrel the size of a rabbit) nosed for food, and from time to time a large regal golden tegu lizard emerged from the bushes on parade.

Nearer to Port of Spain, are the Caroni Inland Waterways – twenty square miles of mangrove wetlands. Every morning some forty thousand scarlet ibis, Trinidad's national bird, leave to feed on the coast of Venezuela. In the evening, at sundown, they return, in vast flocks. A fleet of flat-bottomed boats takes visitors through the complex system of channels to a central lake. There we sat, fallen into silence, waiting for the sun to go down. The birds came, one by one, and then in flocks, black on the horizon, turning vibrant scarlet as they gracefully swooped in to land. They folded their wings and flocked in trees, dotting the branches like chattering red Christmas decorations. On neighbouring trees blue egrets distributed themselves, settling down for the night; an adjoining island was snowy with white egrets. Slowly as the sun set, and the sky turned pink, silence descended on the bird-filled islands and the barges chugged their way home through eerie mangrove swamps in the dark.

Star's time in quarantine was slowly coming to an end. Incarcerated in his little pen, he had learned to do very small mad-fits of welcome every day when I arrived, laden with treats and toys. But the welcome capers became smaller and smaller. He was not well. His skin had broken out in a staphylococci infection. I dosed him with everything I knew, but nothing seemed to work. The kennel vet put him on a strong antibiotic, against my better judgement. It was against Star's judgement too; he spat them out whenever he could. He began to lose his taste for life – and for food. One day I gave him a fine dish of freshly cooked mince, which he wolfed down in best bull terrier style, and then lay down, obviously in agonising digestive pain. He lost his colour, if a white dog can be said to do so, and began to look transparent. We worried that he would not survive this imprisonment.

'He's fine!' said the quarantine vet. 'We've done some tests.'

But Star turned away sadly from food, even his favourite Rask biscuits, and went into his kennel.

Squirrel, the once thin little kennel cat, was at home, eating and growing fat. He had never had so much food in his life. He loved his new life, his toys and all the affection. He grew to twice the size, his coat and tail thickened, and he became a beauty. He was no longer a scrawny squirrel but a glamorous chocolate box cat with huge green eyes. A white half-Persian, he had patches of tabby and grew a pair of magnificent whiskers to match his new girth. He was a cheerful little cat but, with the gain in weight and beauty, he also gained in audacity. He thought he was the head of the household. He would open doors by leaping at the handles and, while keen to be petted, would attack KJ from behind, quite fiercely, with claws. It was time for a little visit to the vet. After his operation he seemed shocked. He wasn't sure what had happened, but he crawled on to my lap and stayed there for a long, long time. He resumed his life at a slightly slower pace. As my friend Mary remarked in a letter from London, 'That operation improves males so much – it should be done more often!'

We had a visit from an affable Australian yachtsman. Murray Raynes was a weather-beaten ex-pilot who was sailing solo around the world. He was following the Test cricket matches around the Caribbean at the time. Full of stories and good Aussie jokes he entertained us on his yacht. We sailed 'down de Islands' – the little string of islands which are the tail end of the Andes in the north of Venezuela. Some are semi-inhabited, some have holiday houses, and all of them are favourite weekend destinations for Trinidadians who migrate across the water clutching rum punch and cool-boxes. We sailed out of the marina at Chagaramas, and into the open sea, anchoring near Chacachacare Island, once a leper colony run by nuns. The rocky island was sad and eerie, much as it had been left when the colony was disbanded; even to open filing cabinets and medical records strewn on the floor. The last leper died in 1984. We wondered about the lives that had been lived there and saluted the heroic nuns. As night fell we chatted and swam, and cooked in the tiny galley kitchen. The last swim was late at night, and our limbs glowed with magical phosphorescence. It was a night of the full moon. Every time I woke, the moon swayed crazily like a ball on a string as the ship swung on its anchor.

In return we invited Murray to a pre-Christmas cocktail party. It was a big affair, in the garden of the house. There were steel pan players at the gate and Living Water ladies serving refreshments. Murray had been forewarned. This would be Trinidad in Sunday best. He thought he had a jacket somewhere but wasn't sure about shoes after a barefoot year on his yacht. When he arrived he was resplendent in long trousers, a sports jacket and even an old school tie. I peeped at his feet. Yes, he had found some shoes. But as the evening wore on the strain began to show. Every so often he eased a foot out of one or the other as he talked. At the end of the night he welcomed the chance for some exercise and walked back to his yacht in the port. As soon as he was outside the curly iron gates of the house he took off his shoes, and walked along, swinging them by the laces as he looked for the nearest dustbin in which to deposit them forever. Who knows whether he ever wore shoes again?

Meantime, back at the house, Mitzi, the little black dog from the park, was thriving. She was fat and happy. She still had her suspicions of ladders and workmen in overalls but life was good. If Star was coming home, it would not be fair to either of them and she would need a new home. Dr Rahaman, the kindly vet in Maraval, patron of Trinidad's gentle street dogs, offered to help. He had large kennels attached to his surgery where employees looked after the boarders. Since Star was almost due to come out of quarantine, we arranged to pay Mitzi's 'board' there until a new home could be found. In only a few days we were telephoned. Mitzi had a home! She was going to live the life of Riley with the Solicitor General whose daughter loved animals. Even better, we would see them quite often at cocktails and functions and could ask about her. I went to the kennels to say goodbye to her. She was clean and fluffy and glowing with health. Her eyes were bright, she was mischievous and prancing and happy. Better still, she loved the kennel employees who looked after her – even though they wore orange overalls. She was a rehabilitated dog. For the remainder of our time in Trinidad, we made a beeline for the Solicitor General and his wife every time we saw them at grand cocktail parties, dinners and balls. They always knew what was coming. Catching their eye, we would dash across to greet them, exchange pleasantries, and then say: 'By the way, how's Mitzi?'

Murray the yachtsman reappeared. He had had boat trouble in Barbados and needed to return for repairs to the Trinidad marina. There was a rather grand invitation to a cricket match as guests of one of the many international oil companies working on the island. We had never been to a match before. My father had been an aficionado, and used to risk divorce by staying up all night in Australia, his ear glued to the radio when the Test matches were played at Lord's, but I only had the most basic idea of the game. KJ, an Irishman, knew even less. Australia was playing the West Indies. We asked for an extra ticket so that Murray could come along on condition that he answered all our silly questions. It was an enlightening day. The cricketers astonished us with their athleticism and skill. I realised how tactical a game it was, like chess. The sun shone. The seller of roasted peanuts sang his wares and tossed bags of nuts into the crowds. Every time a six was hit a clip of a madly dancing baby cavorted on a giant screen and bikini-clad lovelies dived into a rubber blow-up pool in one of the stands. When a wicket fell the crowd rose to its feet in unison as though pulled up by a string. We were served snacks courtesy of the oil company every time we looked around. We went home as the sun was setting feeling replete.

When we arrived home I called Squirrel. He usually came. This time he did not. I looked in all his usual places and round the garden and called some more, then went in and waited for him to reappear. I had seen him at 6 a.m. when I gave him his breakfast. He had eaten it, and happily made for the garden. The watchman had seen him too. And that was the last anyone saw of Squirrel. I scoured the neighbourhood, put notices on trees and advertisements in the paper. Photographs were put up at all the vets, we visited pet shops, radio calls were made, a picture was even flashed up on Trinidad TV, to the incredulity of the announcer. Various calls were received, all leading nowhere and most of them hoping for a reward for no information. We walked the streets at night for weeks, calling his name, and drove heart in mouth to inspect reported bodies of cats – none of them Squirrel. He was so beautiful – our only conclusion was that he had been stolen. With his fluffy coat, his huge green eyes and his little red collar he was obviously a pet. What sort of person could do this? Didn't they know what grief it would cause? Would they care? We could only hope he would be happy and cared for.

After six long months of political imprisonment Star was free at last. He had been kindly treated by the kennel attendants, of that there was no doubt. But he had been bewildered and lonely and he was ill. He came out of incarceration, an old white shadow of the dog who had scampered so joyously while we packed in Suriname. It was as if he could not believe that at last he had the sun on his back. He got out of the car and slowly went to sniff the green grass. It was not concrete. Then he lay down on the lawn, stretching himself out so that every bit of his body was in healing contact with the earth. He laid there for a long time, unbelieving – white dog against the green lawn.

As the days went by he cheered up. We took him to vet. He went to Dr Rahaman, who suggested taking him off all medication to see what happened. He was seen by the entire veterinary faculty at the auspiciously named Mount Hope University. He was introduced to the students by Dr John Watkins, their Welsh professor – 'I want you to meet a real English bull terrier!' – and they all fell in love with him. Neera Gopee, a tiny, fine-boned Indian vet, was his special friend who hugged him and brought him water when he arrived. His ECG was sent to Miami for interpretation. He went to see a special alternative doctor who sent him to see a special alternative vet in San Fernando. Dr Hussein, wearing white shorts and black socks, put Star on his examining table and gazed at him reflectively.

'Now what am I seeing?' he said.

What he was seeing was an eight-year-old dog who looked old. His once massive and muscular frame had lost its tone and spring, his face was thin and his eyes were sad. He no longer had any skin complaints; the antibiotics had wiped them out, and they had wiped out his colour, his spirit and his *joie de vivre*. His liver was poisoned and damaged, his lungs were awash with fluid, and his lion heart was grossly enlarged.

Star had many visits to vets. He had everything at home that could make his life happy. One day he chewed a dustbin and we rejoiced. He was prescribed and liked small tins of cat food. Much to my delight he would purloin them from the cupboard and try to open them with his teeth. KJ was bailed up and had his hand luggage searched at Heathrow airport when be brought twenty tins through the security gates. At night we would go for a pre-bedtime walk in the garden. Under the moonlight the dew-wet grass had become an obstacle course, studded with large frogs and huge fist-sized Caribbean snails. Small frogs chirped in the trees.

Christmas came. Star had lost heart and he turned away from turkey. The cat food lost its appeal. We tried coconut water and baby food. We went for walks in the garden. He began to falter and fall with mini heart attacks. At night he slept on his cushion in the kitchen, with healing tonal music playing on a loop, in a desperate hope that somehow it might help. I crept down the stairs several times a night to be with him. He began to eat pebbles and small stones and his feet were constantly cold.

One morning he went into the garden. It was KJ's birthday. Star walked under the banana trees, among the red and yellow heliconias, sniffing the air. As he walked, one tiny green hummingbird accompanied him, hanging suspended above his head, as though attached by an unseen cord. We tried to hug life into him. His stomach was hard. We called the vet.

'Bring him!' he said.

En route, Star stargazed out the window. He saluted a young Rottweiler jaunting effortlessly down the road on dog business.

Once in the surgery, he lay down on the table, sighing with relief.

'It's time,' said the vet.

Through my tears I could only say, 'Whatever's best for Star.'

He was given a sedative and a fatal injection.

'He's gone,' said the vet.

'No,' I said. 'He's here!' At that moment a burst of light seemed to engulf us, spreading a metre round from the little body on the table.

We took him home with honour, and stayed with him, stroking and murmuring to the little hovering soul so that he knew he was loved. When he grew cold, we buried him, under the 'Fairy Tree' the 'Pride of Barbados' with its clusters of fiery red flowers, rich with nectar.

Star went, as did all our dogs, shrouded like a pharaoh, and supplied with squeaky toys for the next life. As he lay there a little girl called Anna cosied him with flowers, furry red pussycat tails, and said goodnight. We covered him in earth, and sat in silence. And as we sat, there in the Fairy Tree, the Pride of Barbados, a black bird began to sing, endlessly, not drawing breath, drawing the sadness out of us in the thread of melody, swirling our souls with his.

For a while it was as if light pervaded the house and garden. All the desperate love and care that had been poured out on to this little creature hovered in the air like a great dome. For months I lit a lamp on the grave at night, as they do in Sweden, so that the Angel of Light would care for him. I gathered patterned stones and surrounded the grave with them. Sitting with my feet on the rocks, it was as if a vibration travelled up from the earth. Others felt it too.

As time went on, the sorrow lessened, although his grave was always hung with coloured lights when we had parties. Just to include him. But from then on, an odd thing began to happen. Stray animals began to come into the garden. We found a tiny Pomeranian with a deceptively fierce-looking under bite sitting in a garden bed, wandered in from a house several streets away. We cared for her overnight, marvelling at her fragility and affection, put notices on a tree and found her owner. A second black Trinidadian pompek came to be cared for. Cats and kittens appeared in the garden. Some stayed. A manicou, a cat-sized rodent with a long tail and pointed nose, moved in and lived under the house. Was Star's spirit perhaps giving them the message that it was a place of safety? We wondered.

9

'Here Every Creed and Race
Find an Equal Place!'*

Life in the house was lively. Beverley arrived every morning like a noisy ray of sunshine, delighted with her success in buying fresh fruit and vegetables at the fruit stall down the road. No more three-metre long beans as in Suriname, but now we had christophine, dasheen and sorrel. We had to learn to call eggplant melongene, chive was saive, and okra was ochroes. And we made the acquaintance of Chadon Beni, that pungent Trinidadian herb that grew like weeds in the garden and tasted like coriander. Beverley was filled with energy. She moved like a whirlwind through the house. She cleaned and polished everything in sight every day, cooked lunch, did the washing, washed the kitchen floor and departed with a cheerful flurry in the early afternoon to live her own life. It seemed too much for one person. We asked if she would like someone to help her and, as we usually did, gave her the chance to find someone she could work with. And that was how we met Marisa.

Marisa was the girlfriend of one of Beverley's three sons – the one who was a fanatical steel pan player. She was a member of the group known in Trinidad as the FBI – or 'Fine-boned Indians' – a tall delicate girl, with breakable, slender, fragile limbs and enormous eyes. When she came for her interview she was so overcome by shyness that she could not utter a word. Her only remark came when asked why she wanted to work with us. It was not helpful. She said: 'I don't know.'

---

* Refrain of Trinidad and Tobago National Anthem

We exchanged glances, thinking, 'This isn't going anywhere,' but Beverley in her jolly way was confident that she could teach the new recruit. For the first few weeks Marisa was no more than a silent shy smile in the house. But slowly she became a palpable entity. I was aware of laughter in the kitchen, and a delicate presence, a shadow holding the right kitchen implement and spiriting impeccable ironing into the cupboards. The table was scrupulously set, and at my side, a slim figure watched the arranging of flowers or the garnishing of a dish with eyes hungry to learn. Marisa was a treasure. She and Beverley formed a team, more like sisters than mother and daughter-in-law. They were ecstatic at the prospect of choosing materials and being measured for new uniforms. When the smart suits arrived they danced together around the kitchen, admiring each other.

Beverley's love of cooking found its outlet in KJ's lunches. 'My cha cha chicken' was joined by 'my fish stew', 'my callaloo', and 'my lamb chops in soya and honey' as firm favourites. The staff loved to joke, they loved little surprises, and enjoyed introducing us to local delicacies. They specially loved to be the first to tell KJ of any small dramas of the morning. Teenager-like they would rush to greet him, bursting with news of the latest domestic mini-drama.

In the garden was Krishna, and who could resist thinking of him as The Lord? (It was even more tempting since my hairdresser was 'Vishnu' as well.) Krishna the gardener was a bright light of the Maraval Golf Club and coached aspiring players. He shared the Trinidadian passion for cricket – this, after all, was the land of Brian Lara. In Trinidad, when the Test series was on, the score boomed from public address systems, meetings stopped dead when the ball was hit for six, supermarket shelves spoke the scores and solemn men in suits were glued to tiny radios.

On Sundays, with family and friends, Krishna repaired with his friends for a day at the beach in Chagaramas. While the men staged an impromptu beach cricket match, the ladies laboured to produce a gargantuan spicy lunch.

He was not quite so passionate about gardening. An engaging scamp, he could all too often be found asleep in the shade. But eventually, with encouragement, and in Krishna's own time, things would be weeded and planted.

As in other places, the office employed several drivers. KJ's driver, Earl – he of the ready smile and the fast speech – was a firm friend. He would tuck any request into his itinerary for the day, helped everyone and never forgot a commission. Driver number two, Jerome, was a tall, soft-spoken man who lived in Laventille, the roughest and most feared area of Port of Spain. His eyes smiled behind their glasses. With encouragement he could launch into an imitation of some of Trinidad's best comedians. Driver number three lived 'in South' – almost an hour's drive away in the second city, San Fernando. He augmented his income by using his private car as an unofficial taxi service. Mr Nunez, as he was always known, was a pleasant fellow, though like Macavity, the Mystery Cat, he had a certain talent for not being there. His job description included the appellation 'handyman'. When called upon in this capacity, he could indeed do repairs of all kinds. But it took time. Sometimes a very long time. When called, he would arrive at the kitchen door, and, an hour later, I would go down to find that he had been entertaining Beverley – 'Jus liming.' Somehow, Mr Nunez always seemed to arrive without his hammer and toolkit. It would then be necessary to disappear for half a day to find it. An ardent churchgoer, he had strict ideas about correctness. One day he was called in to repair a bathroom tap that had broken. I showed him to the bathroom and he went in. Almost immediately he shot out again, one hand theatrically in front of his eyes.

'There is something in there,' he said, 'that MUST NOT BE SEEN!'

I went in to investigate and found that, in the shower recess, some of my racier underwear was hanging out to dry.

Workmen in Trinidad were often a source of delight. The house was old and had been designed with a slatted gap above the doors to encourage a through draught of air. Modern ducted air conditioning had been installed, but like many things in Trinidad, it had a tendency to expire when overtaxed, and always in the hottest weather. One day when this happened yet again the house was filled with an air conditioning crew. We tripped over them in every room as they climbed ladders, or crawled on hands and knees to check ducts and pipes. When I brought them some iced water one of them was missing. No one knew where he was. Finally he was found – sound asleep in the sauna conditions of the ceiling. His friend was sitting on a ladder at the top of the stairs before lunch. After lunch he was still sitting in the same place.

'What are you doing there?' I asked. He looked at me as if it should be perfectly obvious.

'I waitin' for de duck to drip!'

'Duck to drip?' What…?

It was another one of those moments. Fortunately by that time, I had been studying the Trini form of English for a while. Translation: 'I'm waiting for the duct to drip.' Of course.

Not so delightful was the firm of gardeners called in to enrich the soil with a load of compost. I walked around with the boss, as we discussed the number of bags of fertiliser that would be required. On the way round the garden he made various 'helpful' suggestions as to what could be done with the garden to which I was, I thought, non-committal, having no intention of making any changes whatsoever.

The next day I went to the supermarket. On my return Beverley ran to meet me.

'The gardeners are here!' she shouted. 'They cutting everything! They destroying the garden!'

I rushed to look. There they were, a team of men, hacking, sawing, pruning and demolishing. The wreckage of greenery and bushes lay on the lawn.

'Stop!' I bellowed just as yet another tree branch came crashing down. 'What do you think you're doing?'

'We jus' carryin' out de plan!' was the reply.

I was speechless. The lush garden lay in ruins around our feet, shady areas were open to the sky, and worst of all, several birds' nests had come down with the tree branches, and were reposing full of chicks on the ground, no doubt leaving their mothers distraught. Trying to think of a way to save them I picked up a nest and a baby bird promptly fluttered down to earth. The boss of the gardening firm sent one of his men home to fetch some nests. He arrived back with a few hanging baskets neatly lined with a sort of padded duvet for birds. This had obviously happened before. The nests were tenderly placed in these baskets, they were hung on branches, and we retired. I was assured that their mothers would find them. I was not hopeful. But they did. Happily they flew in and out and day by day the chicks diminished in number as they were launched. Finally the nest baskets were empty. The gardeners were paid – less than they had planned – and, in time, the garden grew back, though never to its former lushness.

When the electricity failed, Mr Kirwen de la Motte was called in. Obviously a descendent of one of the families of early French settlers in Trinidad, Kirwen was a tall, serious gentleman who had immense pride in his work. Nothing was too much trouble and no matter how long it took, he would find the source of the problem. He was particularly proud of his achievements in setting up coloured lights for Europe Day and other large outdoor functions. Spotlights would be beamed on the flags, KJ's lectern would be illuminated, and lights would be threaded through palm trees and hedges. So proud was he of his work and so determined that everything would work efficiently that he would don dinner suit and black tie, so as to mingle unobtrusively and in a fitting manner with the guests, just in case there should be a blackout or short circuit and his services might be required.

Kirwen had a disabled daughter. Tiny, pretty and not very mobile, she had the personality of a Type-A achiever, and in the most charming way, saw no reason why she should not achieve anything she wanted. 'I could be Miss Universe!' she said grandly. Her current desire, though was more modest. She wanted to swim in our pool, which she did. She also needed a new wheelchair to suit her minuscule proportions and this was worrying her father a great deal. In any normal wheelchair she slipped down so far as to be invisible. As usual, there was an association of the Wives of Heads of Mission in Port of Spain. We organised a series of imaginative fund-raising activities which, in the lively social scene of Trinidad, raised serious money. With a little judicious talking, a wheelchair could be placed on the next list of projects. After the chair was acquired, the glory of the outdoor lighting at our garden functions knew no bounds. Kirwen not only wore his black tie, but would cheerfully have camped out overnight in the garden to ensure that all would go well.

All generally did go well. In Trinidad most things were obtainable. The kind of crisis that made for so many funny stories in Africa was less frequent and it was easier on the nerves. After living in Angola and Suriname it was a relief to go into the large supermarkets and the well-stocked shopping malls, and to find locally made goods from the industrial sites, goods from England, from the US, from Canada, India and many other places. And if something was not available at the supermarkets there was a small chain of shops called 'Peppercorns' which prided itself on stocking the non-obtainable. Peripheral requirements were easy too. Trinidad was full of brightly coloured textiles for clothes and decoration, there were hire companies for everything imaginable, there was a multiplicity of music shops and recording studios due to Carnival, music groups and choirs abounded, and, as in Suriname, flowers were abundant.

In Suriname we went to the Javanese flower sellers on their trucks outside the Torarica Hotel for flowers. In Port of Spain we went to the Scout Hall. Just off the Savannah, near the zoo, Lady Chancellor Road wended its way up Poui Hill. Halfway up on the left was a small Scout Hall. There, from Wednesday to Saturday, from 6 a.m. until midday, the ladies of the Horticultural Society sold flowers. And what flowers! The hall was filled with buckets of multicoloured orchids, white, yellow, heliotrope, pink and russet. There were heliconias – red and orange parrot beaks, graceful pink, flamingo-like 'Sexy Pinks' drooping from their stems, and contorted russet and green 'Twisted Sisters' like hula dancers undulating their hips. There were bunches of ornamental banana flowers, and sometimes the crunchy white flowers of the yukka palm. Porcelain roses budded, pale in their virginal pinks, and buckets of tuberose swooned in their own heady perfume. But above all there were anthuriums, their waxy lily shapes bunched together in colour-coded buckets – deep wine red, almost black, anthuriums, tiny stiff pink flowers like shiny little cats' tongues, brilliant vermillion, cream and white, pale red with tinges of green and the queen of them all, the beautiful obaki, with its long pointed blooms like the ears of a rather large elf, exquisitely shaded in delicate pinks and greens.

The Ladies of the Horticultural Society were the Trinidadian version of the Women's Institute in every land. Middle-aged and comfortable, they loved what they did. Trinidad and Tobago is a major exporter of tropical flowers to America and Europe, and the ladies gathered in their Scout Hall the flowers that were surplus to growers' requirements, flowers and greenery from private gardens, fruit in season – even occasional cakes and pies. It was a cosy cornucopia presided over by the kindly, fun-loving brown ladies and their tea trays. And on the tea trays pecking the bowls of sugar, perched bright golden orioles.

For a ridiculously small sum, I would emerge from the Scout Hall, satiated with colour and drunk on flower shopping – laden with armfuls of beauty to be sorted and arranged into vases. Beverley and Marisa would be waiting and together we would happily combine and create a dozen vases of flowers, needing nothing but the perfect colour and line of the blooms.

Flower day was often Thursday, which was the day the meditation group met in the house. The meditation group had become a tradition and a part of life. I had learned to be 'upfront' about this interest. In the beginning, I had been reticent about it, expecting to be judged as lunatic fringe. As I accepted the role of 'Diplomatic Spouse' I decided to be myself as well. When asked what I did – which was not all that frequent – I would say, 'I'm interested in meditation. I run groups and teach people how to meditate.' This proved to be a less frightening gambit than saying that I was a psychologist, and far from alienating anyone, inevitably brought forward the response.

'How interesting. I've always wanted to learn. Can I come?'

It had all started in Zimbabwe when a discussion group had formed after an unexpected lecture given by Karl Rahner. In Angola, daily meditation had been an essential survival technique. In Swaziland a large group met in the beautiful house on the Malagwane Hill. Our large African tabby Paddycat would line up outside the door on a Monday evening, insisting on taking his place in the circle. When we opened our eyes at the end he would be sitting with us, eyes closed, gently swaying from side to side. When we did t'ai chi, he wove himself in patterns around our feet. In Suriname, a group met in my study, a multi-faith mixture of people. We combined Western, Hindu and Buddhist traditions, with the occasional mixture of ancient shamanic wisdom thrown in from time to time. We ended with tea, coffee, cake and a mixture of gossip and consciousness-raising.

In Trinidad another group formed. Initially it was drawn from the expat community. As time went on, one expat lady after another dropped out, too busy with manicures and mah-jong. A series of Trinidadian voices telephoned to see if they could join. By the end of the time in Trinidad we became a group of a dozen friends, ranging through all the colours, appearances and racial groups of the island's population. We shared our times of intense and healing silence, and tracked each other through life events. The first meditation group baby was welcomed, members were supported through bereavement and through breast cancer. We cooked for each other on birthdays and farewells and went on beach excursions. We discussed everything – including race. Prunella, a golden-skinned young woman with elegant oriental eyes and fair hair revealed that she had endured racial prejudice twice in her life – once at school in Trinidad when she was regarded as being 'too white', and once, later on in Canada when she was 'too dark'. The group reflected all the variety of Trinidad. Sylvia, the darkest skinned among us, was urbane and soignée and a leading light in the United Kingdom Women's Association. Little Irish Katie, who always arrived like a little girl coming late to a birthday party, was married to an Indo-Trinidadian and was a well-known portrait painter. Mica, another artist, with her Pre-Raphaelite mop of strawberry-blonde hair and her background in the Parisian world of fashion, designed trendy clothes and taught t'ai chi in the botanical gardens. Brenda, tall and rangy, ate salads and sailed boats. Marlene, who followed a Buddhist spiritual path, ran one of the largest marinas in Trinidad with her husband and power-walked in her spare time. Trinidad – and meditation – could embrace us all.

As in Suriname, spirituality of all kinds flourished on the island. Christian adherents had been predominantly Catholic from the times of Spanish and French settlement. Catholic churches were full to overflowing on Sundays, but there was also a large Anglican cathedral in town. The Anglican archbishop was a dignified Trinidadian gentleman with a rich reverberating voice and a Lambeth Palace accent. There were unexpected pockets of Presbyterianism in the south of Trinidad among the East Indian population but twenty-two per cent of the population was Hindu. Islam at five per cent was smaller in numbers but influential. The Shouter, or Spiritual, Baptists and the Orisha groups bore witness to traditional West African influences surviving since the days of slavery, now melded into new, syncretic forms of worship.

Interest in spiritual matters was keen. Alison, from England, a modern shamanic practitioner, paid a visit. Trinidad was familiar with this traditional kind of healing. A radio interview was arranged for her with a phone-in question time. We made the mistake of giving a home phone number. The phone was already ringing loudly as we arrived back home. It rang non-stop for an hour, as clients phoned for consultations until, with our eyes standing out on alarmed stalks, we took it off the hook. Alison worked herself to exhaustion during her week-long stay, as clients swarmed through the gate. Rainforest healer Olof visited from Suriname. A series of talks was arranged for him too. So many people flocked to see him that he set up a practice in a small flat and began making his herbal remedies there.

Dr Harry Ramnarine was discovered through a tape of harmonious music playing in a jeweller's showroom. Everyone, it seemed, had heard about Harry. Half of Trinidad seemed to have consulted him or learned from him at some time in their lives. He was a doctor trained in Western medicine. Some thirty years ago he had decided to treat his patients using alternative methods – herbal remedies, vitamins, homeopathy, flower essences, massage, colour and vibrational medicine. The change was far from being professional suicide. His clinic in Chaguanas, south of Port of Spain, was booked up three months in advance. Such was his reputation for cures that patients queued from 6 a.m. every morning to see him. Of course we were intrigued. We made an appointment.

The clinic was off the main highway, along a straight, flat road lined with white houses and vegetable stalls. The waiting room was simple in the extreme – a few wooden benches on a shaded porch. Sundry shoes and sandals reposed by the concrete steps, indicating that very civilised Indian habit of removing shoes before entry. When the doctor emerged he was the owner of the largest pair of sandals, a tall, slim, straight-backed man wearing a dark brown open-necked shirt and glasses. His eyes behind the glasses were deep and reflective but at the edges of his mouth hovered a perpetual smile. He was relaxed, yet wore armour of self-containment, commitment and seriousness – having attained near guru status, perhaps he needed some kind of protection from the worship of his more devoted patients.

The consulting room was one of many small rooms in the house, all painted in vibrant, rich colours – green, blue, purple, deep pink. The walls were covered with charts and lined with books, the desk and shelves crowded with objects. Harry tested the entire physical system down to cellular level. In the centre of Port of Spain itself he had opened a second clinic on the Savannah. Called 'Lightwave 2012', it was a cool and peaceful place. 'Sound and Light' treatments were given. Clients were treated under space-age machines which radiated colours of the spectrum on to the skin. They lay on couches as co-ordinated sound and light waves were beamed via headphones while a slightly alarming 'Startrek' light dome flashed above their heads. Oxygen treatment completed the sessions. We may not all have fully understood the principles behind the treatments but a session of light-wave therapy put wings on the feet and gave a glow inside and out. People began to ask me what the beauty treatment was.

The wings on my feet may have been metaphorical ones but

we woke up one morning in March to find that one much loved resident of Port of Spain had taken wing and departed in the night. The Catholic Archbishop Anthony Pantin had died in his sleep in March 2000. He epitomised the warmth, inclusiveness and humanity of Trinidad at its best. Those who heard the news stood in tears, transfixed in the street. Radio stations were jammed with telephone calls from people wanting to share their memories of the archbishop. And in the succeeding days until his funeral, it seemed that everyone had their 'archbishop' story.

Housekeeper Beverley was a typical example. As a little girl, her mother had to work hard and she was deposited outside her convent school at 6 a.m., long before the other children arrived. Every morning the archbishop came to say Mass and was given breakfast by the nuns. Every morning he would stop to talk to the little tot waiting outside and without fail, he would bring her a piece of fruit from the breakfast table. Beverley never forgot his kindness. People told of innumerable examples of humanity, understanding and benevolence, and his capacity to remember people and their circumstances. His schedule was punishing. He woke every morning at 3 a.m., said his prayers, picked up the first newspaper and then spent the time writing, and tape-recording letters until it was time for Mass at 5.30 a.m. And many of the letters were inspired by the day's news. The archbishop would go through the paper, noting who was bereaved, who was in trouble, who had succeeded in some way and would write notes of comfort, help or congratulation. Status, social group, culture or religious affiliation was no bar to his humanity. He was as likely to take off his shoes and pray in a Hindu temple as to play games with the children who visited him in his house with its open door. Anthony Pantin was born on the island and spoke with a Trini accent in the down to earth and humorous local idiom. In his early days as archbishop he chose to live, not in the archbishop's house, but in Laventille – the hillside community infamous for its gangs, delinquents and drug dealers. He described those years as the happiest time of his life.

'I love people,' he said. 'I love being with the people. And I don't like them to be in trouble.'

As the TnT (Trinidad and Tobago) News Network put it: 'Dis one shock de country yesterday...Archbishop Anthony Pantin dead in he sleep on Sat night/Sun mornin'...de doctors tell him he okay now and jus' take it easy for ah while...he was back at work again...an' den jus' so de man dead boy! When yuh number call, it really call, eh. But he certainly leave he mark t'ough...he was always ah fella for tolerance, racial unity, respect for all religions, use tuh have people comin' by he house regularly tuh get ah handout, you coulda pick up yuh phone an' call him, and he woulda talk tuh yuh...yuh didn't have tuh be "somebody"...if is one 'ting people sayin' all over de place...even if you didn't agree wit' what de fella say, yuh know wey he stand on any issue...an' like true Trini he had ah good sense of humour an' enjoy ah good time. What ah could say...in we own way...dat was ah good fella!'

The day of the funeral was sunny and hot, like most days in Port of Spain. We saw a procession of pennants on long lances apparently sailing along the top of our garden wall. It was the mounted police escort coming from their headquarters on Long Circular Road in formation. Smart in their starched white uniform jackets and helmets, they crossed the Wildflower Park and disappeared in the direction of the archbishop's house. From there they would escort the body in its black hearse through the streets. Schoolchildren lined the route. Steel pan players dressed in black played their salute as the coffin passed. There was a solid phalanx of singing, waving, tearful Trinidadians along the route to say their farewells. At the cathedral a group of African drummers welcomed him. There was an all-night vigil in the cathedral. For an entire day thousands of people filed past the open coffin – people of all ages, ranks, cultures and social classes, not only Catholics, not only Christians (this was Trinidad after all), but Muslims, Hindus and those who no longer knew what they believed, but had known the archbishop's kindness.

After the second night's vigil the funeral began on Saturday morning. It was held on the cathedral forecourt and a stage was erected so that the thousands who gathered in Brian Lara Promenade could take part. Priests and bishops from the region were there in their finery. But it was the people who were mourning their own archbishop.

At the end of the ceremonies, the national flag was taken from the coffin by policewomen, folded neatly and handed to the family. As the coffin was carried in procession to the crypt a steel pan band played 'Be Still My Soul', reducing anyone who was still dry-eyed to tears. The coffin was lowered into the crypt, and bricked in by a worker dressed in a black suit. An Irish priest sang 'The Holy City'. The presiding priest's voice broke into a sob when he announced that the crypt had finally been sealed.

'What ah could say...in we own way...dat was ah good fella!'

10

Around the World in Forty Days

It was now the year of the millennium. The world was supposed to come to an end, computers might crash globally and bring down entire financial empires with them. Planes might fall out of the sky. Being human, those of us who were not praying decided to party anyway and the event was celebrated for twenty-four hours around the globe with ceremonies and fireworks. When we all realised that midnight had passed and nothing disastrous had happened, we went to bed.

To celebrate KJ's birthday we had planned to go round the world. If a knitting needle were to be stuck through the globe in the Caribbean it would come out somewhere in Australia. If we were going to visit my mother anyway, a round the world ticket was no further and no more expensive than going there and back.

We began by taking a plane from Trinidad to Miami. Miami airport is now regarded by some as the new capital of Latin America. It is full of Spanish speakers rushing hysterically in all directions, all festooned with multiple bags and dragging large families of multi-sized children. For a bit of peace, we followed up a tip in a brochure and went to the tenth floor of a hotel bizarrely situated in the middle of the airport concourse. There we found a gym and a swimming pool and disported ourselves for an hour. En route to the British Airways boarding gates we made another discovery. Along one of the passageways was an area of magic colour therapy. There were floor-to-ceiling windows in the colours of the spectrum, and, as passengers glided through on a moving belt, little oriental bells chimed. If only such stress relief could be cloned and applied by law in all airports worldwide.

Going the long way round, we had a brief sojourn in an unusually sunny Britain, and set off on the long haul to Singapore. Changi airport was dripping with fountains and festooned with orchids and we delighted in the teams of workers who creep in at midnight, to pick off every spent bloom from the plants. We set off for the Newton Road outdoor food market. All the smells and possibilities of Asian food wafted into our nostrils. After the chilli crab we went in search of any stray cats who might live in the bushes. Armed with an extra helping of white fish we crouched in the undergrowth, waiting to see what would happen. First a little black and white cat appeared, then her three kittens clustered round the fish and noodles. A small ginger tabby arrived and tucked in. When they were all eating we noticed a movement at the side. A tiny white form appeared. It was a torpedo-shaped, bewhiskered white mouse with a very long snout. He – or she – lined up with the cats and kittens and began nibbling too. It was as if all of these little outcasts of the city of Singapore had a pact to live in peace and share whatever good things came their way.

After spending some time with my mother, a sprightly lady of ninety-eight, we planned to visit Sydney. It was the year of the Olympics. Before KJ and I left, Mother and I watched the magical opening of the Olympic Games together on TV. Her chief preoccupation was not how well Australia was appearing on the world stage, but anxiety about how much it must all have cost!

En route to Sydney the couple on the aircraft seats in front of us caroused rather too copiously on Australian red wine, and spilled quite a lot of it on themselves, the seat and on KJ's new white Reeboks. Seeing his new bright pink footwear the hostess was beside herself with efforts at restitution. She came up with an idea. Obviously he would have to attend the Olympics in pink shoes, but to make it all better she presented us with a newspaper parcel containing two bottles of the red wine which had caused the damage. Oddly, the trainers restored themselves to their original colour in a couple of days but we drank the wine anyway.

The Sydney Olympics – what a feast. I had been doubtful about going at all. 'It will be horrendously crowded!' I had said. 'All the pickpockets from the entire southern hemisphere will be there! We won't get tickets!' Then, 'It's too late to book accommodation...!' And so on. But in the event, we did get plane bookings, AND tickets, AND wonderful accommodation in a private house.

From the moment of our arrival at Sydney airport, awash with some of the forty-five thousand cheerful Olympic volunteers in their bright blue-splashed shirts and their Aussie stockman's jackets and hats, we sensed the bubble of childlike excitement that marked the whole event. The air was buzzing with anticipation, like the day before a gigantic birthday party. Welcome, friendliness, helpfulness, super-efficiency, were the words on everyone's lips. The entire population of Sydney seemed bent on enjoying the occasion and making sure all the visitors did too. It was, as one amazed newspaper columnist put it, 'Like a family wedding where we've all promised not to get drunk in front of the in-laws.' And behave themselves the Sydneysiders did. As far as we could see no one complained about anything, or perhaps all the Scrooges had wisely left town. The litterless city had been repainted and spruced up for the occasion – invisible street cleaners apparently worked overtime, the sun sparkled on Sydney Harbour and its innumerable coves. Our first view of the harbour came the very night of our arrival as we were efficiently and miraculously scooped up by name at the airport and placed in a minibus which transported us to the very door of our accommodation. We travelled from the airport through immense tunnels and suddenly came to the surface with a collective 'Oh' as we all saw, for the first time, the lighted Sydney Harbour Bridge and the Opera House, iridescent in changing rainbow lights under the night sky.

For our five days in Sydney, we became complete Aussies, turning on the TV at every possible moment just to see how things were going at the sports stadium, or sneaking a quick look at one of the big screens set up in the open spaces of the city, joining in the jocular chant of 'Aussie, Aussie, Aussie, Oy Oy Oy' (or Hoy Hoy Hoy, when the equestrian Andrew Hoy was performing). We empathised with the triumphs and upsets of athletes from all nations. And while the victories of Australian athletes like Cathy

Freeman and Ian Thorpe caused roof-raising cheers, Australian crowds were quick to honour great performances from any nation, and were generous with their appreciation and support.

Having lapped up the mysticism, poetry, humour and spectacle of the opening ceremony, with its aboriginal rituals and 'dancing dunnys' (old-fashioned backyard lavatories), we were thrilled when the stockman who lead the grand opening charge on to the arena on his great black rearing horse, appeared with his horse and dog at the equestrian centre on the day we attended. He gave a demonstration, laced with dry Aussie humour, of apparent telepathy between his animals and himself. We had seen that figure from the Snowy River legend gallop into the arena with a breathtaking rear, and now we watched him do it again – 'Just wanted to make another entrance in my coat and hat!' – then sat back and enjoyed the antics of man, dog and horse, as they played football together, played tricks on each other, retrieved the stockman's hat from odd places and finally, stood on the tiny winner's rostrum to receive their gold medal.

We saw the best dressage riders in the world, elegant and controlled, going through their routines, their horses dancing and floating over the arena in their half-passes and flying changes, flinging out dainty hooves as they performed equine versions of the skip and polka.

We made the route march to the athletics stadium and formed one of the dots among the other eleven thousand spectators as Cathy Freeman ran one of her heats, and Gail Devers ran out, injured. We cheered ourselves hoarse for Ato Bolden from Trinidad to the amazement of the two solid Trinidadian men on our left, and saw Maurice Greene pacing like a tiger, prior to a flying victory. We marvelled at the military precision of the organisation, as five or six track and field events took place simultaneously, each one with its team of impeccable officials carefully supervising every detail. And we fell in love with the robotic little seeing-eye camera, travelling faster than the runners like a motorised mouse, tracking and photographing their every move, and the little camera capsule that jumped, flea-like, up the posts with every jumper and pole-vaulter, falling back each time as though exhausted by the effort.

At every coming and going, we were helped and encouraged and cheered up by the flotillas of blue and white clad volunteers, waving their red torches at night, pointing out the last toilets before the train 'use it now!', advising parents to write their cell phone numbers on their children's hands in case of straying. 'Branding irons are discouraged!' Guiding the crowds into the easiest lines for good train seats, manning the barricades with a steady flow of banter and good humour – surely there was never an Olympics like this. We felt as if we had stepped into some golden age when human beings had discovered a new realm of co-operation and shared pleasure. Certainly, the food at the stadium was expensive and sometimes we were too cold and sometimes too hot – but these moments passed. What remained was the sense of harmony and good feeling that prevailed.

We saw all sides of Sydney with our hosts. We visited Bondi Beach, ate an Australian meat pie at 'Joe de Wheels' – a mobile pieman patronised, we were told, by celebrities. While harmlessly eating our pie on the waterfront the car was nabbed by a pair of traffic wardens, internationally merciless, despite our invocation of the Olympic spirit. A very tall and corpulent gentleman, in a business suit, saw what was happening, and deftly removed his large black Mercedes from danger. He reappeared when all was quiet, uttering the Dickensian line 'Grubs they are, grubs – the lowest form of life!' as he proceeded to munition himself with a monstrous 'Tiger' pie, peas and mash.

We visited the Sydney Opera House, a long held ambition of mine, and took a tour. Once more we were treated to Australian humour. Our guide was a tall, dark, cadaverous chap with a mastery of deadpan delivery and a fine repertoire of foreign phrases and accents. Perhaps the best moment occurred in the main opera theatre, which was in the midst of a production change. On the stage black-clad stage hands milled about, cleaning.

'You see before you, ladies and gentlemen,' intoned our guide, 'a full rehearsal of the Black Theatre of Prague, shortly to open in a new ballet entitled *Brooms*.' We snorted and wondered whether our co-tourists from non-English speaking countries had got the joke. We didn't see that or any other production. But we did see the stage set for *Troilus and Cressida* in a production by Bogdanov, and were rendered thoughtful by the presence of a great number of ancient Trojan TV sets and a lot of sofas that looked decidedly 1940s.

On our last night in Sydney we ate at a restaurant almost under the bridge, watched the Opera House change colour from turquoise to amethyst, to sunset red and gold, as pleasure craft bedecked with fairy lights plied back and forth and little yachts with stars on their masts glided invisibly into berth. We tried to inscribe the scene on our minds so that two nights later, after we had left, when the 'river of fire' reached the bridge, and all of the Olympic rings of light would explode in rainbow fireworks, we would know how it felt.

We flew on to Honolulu, en route to the US. On our right was a charmingly tweedy and eccentric professor from Melbourne University who seemed to have taken a vow to read his way through every newspaper published in the world that day. As he read he threw each paper loosely on to the floor at his feet, so that by the end of the flight, he had created such a mountain of crumpled newspapers that he all but disappeared under them. Occasionally though, he emerged from under the paper mountain and imperiously beckoned to me in order to point out esoteric facts about islands and reefs and cloud formations along the way. And our charming and quirky steward looked exactly like the actor Nigel Hawthorne but fortunately was a lot less mad than that actor was in *The Madness of King George*.

Honolulu, which we had visited briefly before, has its own special energy and magic. Unfortunately it also has its own special brand of huge, nightmarish freeways populated by hundreds of black-windowed stretch limos, all looking as though they are transporting Mafia groups on the way to an assassination. We felt that we'd done the tourist trail on the last visit – eaten the roast pig and marvelled at the fire-eaters and the rock-divers – so we took advantage of the beach, and the tranquillity, spiked with a little judicious coral shopping.

From Honolulu we went on to Dallas, Texas, as they say, where KJ was due to spend the weekend learning from his wood-work master, Perry McDaniel, using the famous Incra jig. (Learning some new jigs, as he likes to say, which is highly appropriate for an Irishman.) While he was well occupied I travelled on to Houston to stay with Texan friends from Trinidad. We had met when we were all daily visitors to the quarantine kennels in Trinidad, and Judy and I subsequently became tropical fish friends, and gym friends, and various other kinds of friends. When our beloved Star died, they fronted up one day with a touching memorial for his grave – a single star on a pole, specially cast from the mould used on the state buildings in Texas: the Lone Star State. So I 'visited' and saw more than I ever wanted to of Route 15 as we buzzed up and down to various shopping malls. We ate at a succession of restaurants all looking like concrete prisons from the outside: fish restaurants, Mexican restaurants, French restaurants, Italian restaurants, all apparently staffed by the same waiters and waitresses in different costumes. Did they have a hectic life running from one to the other I wondered? I waited for Don and Judy to have a meal at home. They never did. Eventually, early one morning I peeped into a kitchen cupboard. It contained just one jar of instant coffee. Like many Americans, they were a family who 'ate out'.

KJ and I were scheduled to meet at the American Airlines check-in at Dallas airport. What we didn't realise was that Dallas airport has five terminal buildings and about eighteen American Airlines check-in points. And KJ had my ticket. As far as I knew I couldn't get to the gate without finding him first. It took a lot of nervous thinking and asking to plan the campaign. In the end I took myself and my baggage on a round the airport underground train ride, and found that everyone else in the train carriage was lost too. Finally having arrived at the terminal from which the plane to Miami took off I found that my beloved had already checked me in, *in absentia* – this was the days before terrorism – and it only needed photographic identification to be allowed into the inner sanctum of the boarding gates. Hooray for computers.

I should mention that we had been travelling, if not light, then at least with limited luggage. We had one medium suitcase each and one small roll-on.

'That's got to be *it*!' KJ had pronounced when we packed. No shopping. No shoe sales – no more books in the luggage. We couldn't afford excess baggage. So with monumental self-restraint no shopping to speak of was done (except for one absolutely irresistible pair of dark grey sequinned evening sandals, very small, and poked into the deepest corner of my suitcase). Any excess books or papers were posted back home. So I was surprised when, at Miami airport, after the luggage emerged on the carousel, KJ was still waiting around. 'There's something else to come,' he said. Finally a porter emerged through a door with a trolley. On the trolley was a parcel for KJ a metre square, and another long thin package, at least two metres long.

'Tools,' he said, as if that explained everything. 'Saw table!'

If ever a woman could be, I was speechless.

We had to hire one of the very longest stretch limos to get the luggage to the hotel. We propped his saw table up against the crystal decanter and glasses as we went.

This final hotel of the trip was the Intercontinental. KJ had stayed in other branches for various conferences in various countries.

And lo and behold they led them up into the veritable high places, yea as far as the thirty-first floor, inlaid with precious marble and hung with carpets of red and gold, and said: 'Ye shall reside henceforth in the abode of the penthouse suite.' And we looked forth and surveyed all of the quays of Miami, and behold it was very good.

We have to this day no idea how we got these palatial rooms. We certainly hadn't booked them. Perhaps everything else was booked out that day. But we enjoyed them, just regretting that there weren't more of us to spread around and that we were rather too tired to play with the drinks bar, the two monstrous TVs, the two bathrooms and the dining and entertaining area.

The tools and the saw table looked a bit incongruous spread out in all the grandeur.

We walked along the foreshore, watched rollerbladers, visited markets, and marvelled at the array of baseball caps on sale, wondered at the size of some of the tracksuits and admired amethyst crystals three feet tall – rather too large to take back even by KJs new standards. I also visited the holy grail of American womanhood, Victoria's Secret – the secret being, someone once said, that no one over thirty can fit into their lingerie. Back at the penthouse we packed, and with a fond glance to memorise what it had been like, set off for the airport where we fell a victim to the temptation to share a 'cinnabon' with our coffee. An awe-inspiring concoction, this huge, sticky and freshly made bun oozed calories, and went far to explain the size of the tracksuits on sale in the market.

Throughout the trip we were constantly diverted by the cultural differences in airline style. The friendly correctness of British Airways, sometimes laced with cockney chirpiness, the laid-back, jokey style of the Qantas stewards ('If that passenger does that again I'll bite his ears off!') and on this trip, the production-line attitude of the American airline staff with their habit of shoving a plastic bag containing a muffin and a bag of chips at passengers with a 'That's all you'll get!' look. Sometimes standards improved slightly, but reasonably tasty food might be served on plastic plates, warm roasted nuts appeared in paper containers and hot American coffee arrived in gigantic plastic mugs.

This trip was no exception. When we came on board, the blonde bombshell air hostess was resolutely ignoring all oncoming passengers and shouting angrily into a telephone. So we found our seats and watched as a mini-drama unfolded. Airline rules clearly stated that passengers could carry on board two items of hand baggage. But only when flights were not full. In this case the plane was packed and one dismayed passenger after another was curtly relieved of his or her cherished carry-on goods. We sat and watched. People winced as their extra baggage was summarily dispatched down a very steep chute to thump and clatter at the bottom into a waiting receptacle, like a giant garbage bin.

Then our hostesses really swung into action. They belonged to the Chicago gangster school of 'service' and they sashayed up and down the aisles, barking from one side of their mouths. 'Nuts!' and 'Yawantwine!' and 'Yawannadessert!' came at us like machine gun fire as plastic plates and napkins and drinks were flung at clients cowering in their seats. A request for a blanket resulted in one unfortunate lady being covered like a tent as the coverlet descended on her from an overhead locker.

I have to admit that in these circumstances, I became more and more the quiet English lady, and by becoming quieter and quieter, more and more pointedly refined every time I was addressed by one of these harridans, managed to reduce her to a state when she almost remembered her manners by the end of the flight. It's an old schoolteacher's trick. Become quieter in the midst of chaos. It works.

Nevertheless, it was pure joy when we landed in Trinidad and a warm, dark brown velvet Caribbean voice announced over the intercom: 'Ladies an' gentlemen, it's rainin' down there, so you walk with the umbrellas we've left for you at the bottom of the gangway, an' make sure you're very, very careful and don't you slip.' West Indian humanity again! We were home.

Now every four years we will be able to sit down in front of the TV and say, in increasingly quavery voices, 'We were at the Sydney Olympics at the beginning of the century!'

11

Coming to an End

Back in Trinidad we knew that in another year the Trinidadian idyll would end but for now, our second Carnival was upon us. Friends from Suriname came to stay, and 'play Mas'.

Peter Minshall, the 'Master of Mas', had created a new mythical theme for this Carnival. Signed-up members were slightly disappointed to be given either black or white overalls to wear. No sparkles? No robes or bikinis? This was how he expressed his latest vision – a prophecy of hope: 'Mas 2000 will start out Carnival Tuesday morning, one thousand black and one thousand white people, zipped neatly into our aviator suits, ground troops sent in to Port of Spain to make love not war. As we enter the streets of Carnival morning, each armed with a squeezy bottle of our colour in paint, we begin to paint each other. The People of the Black Planet give some of their black to the People of the White Planet, a dab here, a line there, a squiggle, a spurt, dots, circles, suns, moons, and stars. The People of the White Planet give some of their white to the People of the Black Planet, white paint on to black suits. As this mixing-up process goes on, the band approaches a site where the all-out Mas playing takes place…a troop of black suits appears, rolling a huge black sphere; across from them, a huge white sphere appears, pushed by a troop of white suits. Drums and tassa roll, iron beats, bells ring, cymbals clash. As the two spheres meet, they peel open, like celestial fruit, and from within comes an explosion of silver and gold – confetti, glitter, fireworks. Then the whole band, all the People of the Black Planet and all the People of the White Planet, also peel open – unzip sleeves and legs and fronts – and their silver and their gold shines out. Silver paint, gold paint, and glitter, on skin – arms, thighs, faces. Black gives white some of its blackness. White gives black some of its whiteness. Out of this encounter, inner beauty is revealed – in explosions of silver and gold!' What a living metaphor for Trinidad, the rainbow culture. What a vision for a united planet!

As we approached the area of the Savannah where the masque was to take place, Peter Minshall's voice was already booming out from the sound truck, telling the story. It all happened exactly as planned. We were left with an embracing, glittering, dancing crowd that flowed through the streets. Once more Trinidad was being used as the ground for a mythology of humankind. His claim that Mas can be a high art form capable of expressing spiritual truths was revalidated.

This was the mixture and the magic of Trinidad. In more than one way it was a place of black and white. It was a kaleidoscope of colour, race, culture, creativity and beauty. And yet it had its dark side. Every Monday morning the front pages of newspapers were splattered with screaming headlines of murder and violence, tragic domestic and village quarrels where the resolution was by cutlass – or cane-cutter's long knife. The darkness and brutality of the harsh slave past had left its shadow.

Trinidad, like Suriname and most Caribbean islands, has always been a staging post between the South American drug trade and its ready market in the US. The human fallout from the ruthless deals were cared for by organisations such as Living Water in drug rehabilitation schemes. Those who were not so lucky or who had fallen out of society for other reasons became part of the large population of street people. A ragged and bearded man rang at front doors, from time to time, raging at the rich and who could blame him. A small lady with a destroyed life and mind came to the house every week for a bag of food. Aids was making its depredations on the young and sexually active and social services were far from adequate. Stories were heard of gangs and vendettas, and kidnappings occurred. There were places where it would have been foolhardy to venture at night. Earl, KJ's driver, was adamant that we should never stop for anyone at night, no matter what the consequences.

For political and economic reasons these trends have accelerated in recent years and sadly, Trinidad now has a high crime rate. The crimes of kidnapping and murder are driven by gangs and complex internal forces. None of it is directed at visitors, although it would be unlucky to be standing in the way. Trinidadians are still joyous, but they live more carefully now – they are more aware of security, and although they do much what they always did, they do it with an eye to who is walking behind.

We all began to take more care. After the bombing of the American embassy in Kenya, the US embassy in Port of Spain became Fort Knox, with steel gates and concrete barriers. KJ's office, which was next door, was forced to install toughened glass in the windows for fear of fallout. The American residence on Flag Staff Hill too was inspected by security from Washington and stringent measures were put in place. Instead of the sleepy Trinidadian night guard in his box, visitors now had to negotiate an alert sentinel with an intercom who checked whether the guest was expected. Papers were carefully checked. Halfway up the long hillside driveway the car would be stopped again, at a second concrete guardhouse. A large concrete barrier rose from the road to bar the car's progress, and uniformed guards emerged to ask for identification, and to check under the car with a mirror for bombs. It was all very impressive but it meant leaving home a quarter of an hour earlier if there was an American function to attend.

The procedures also rebounded on the American ambassador and his wife. Every time they returned to the house their car had to be checked too, just in case a bomb had been planted while their driver was looking the other way. It would take time to get used to it but they resolved to be patient. Unfortunately it took time for the guards to adjust to the new procedures as well. One day Polly, the ambassador's wife, was returning from her shopping. She negotiated the first guardhouse and set off up the hill to the residence, looking forward to her morning coffee. As she approached the second guardhouse, she slowed down, expecting to be stopped. The young guard on duty realised, just too late, that he should have put up the barrier. He pressed the activating button and the metre-high crash barrier rose from the road – unfortunately directly underneath the car. The ambassador's wife and her car rose into the air in a stately manner, accompanied by a horrible crunching under the chassis. She found herself perched and teetering high on the concrete barrier. The ambassador's wife emerged unscathed, apart from a dent in her dignity, but it did the car no good at all.

We had no such dramatic incidents, and were not expecting to be targeted in any way. Europe was seen as a friend. HQ did, however, employ security guards for all residences. Generally the guards were friendly and cheerful fellows who arrived with their sandwiches and flask, patrolled in an official manner until they were sure our lights were out, and then, no doubt took what naps they could. Some were innocent enough to forget about replacing their patio cushions in the morning. Others stripped for a quick dip in the pool, or looked with lascivious eyes on the avocado tree as the fruit ripened. It was a huge tree, with avocadoes the size of small footballs. When opened the flesh was like pale green clotted cream. We noticed that there were at least twenty large fruits ripening and looked forward to them. I inspected them greedily each day. But somehow, there seemed to be less each time I checked. We had our suspicions, but just to be sure, Krishna climbed up on a ladder with a felt tip and we numbered them. They continued to disappear, but not by number. Finally when we were down to five I happened to look at the guard's chair and table as I went out to the gym very early. There, neatly arranged, was a bowl, a spoon and two hollowed out avocado shells.

The mango tree was another great temptation. In fact, just as Inuits have many words for snow, and Zulus have many words for cows, Trinis have many names for their myriad species of mango: long mango, rose, hog, calabash, manzanilla douxdoux, la brea gyul, turpentine, mangotine, and the queen of mangoes, the Julie. In Tobago the roads are lined with mango trees, they are squashed underfoot and the air smells of mango liqueur. In our garden the Julie mangoes were lush. Of course there were enough to go round, the birds, the large green iguanas and the staff could enjoy as many as we did. Sometimes little boys sat on the wall eating them. When

challenged – 'What are you doing?' – one natural-born young the-
ologian shouted from the tree, 'I'm eating God's mangoes!'

But we did raise an eyebrow when an enterprising team of municipal workers mending the electricity poles swung their cher-
ry-picker crane around so that it lodged in our mango tree just to
make the harvesting easier.

After the sadness of losing Star and Squirrel, we had no animals. We enjoyed the various strays who came to be rescued from
time to time, and left food out for the feral cats. One fellow whom
we christened 'Pug Face' was particularly endearing. He had a very
round face with asymmetrical black and ginger markings on it,
making him so ugly that he was beautiful. He lived under the house
together with the resident long-tailed manicou. In the evenings we
had our own 'bird park' in the garden. We put papaya and crumbs
along a fence, and sat with our tea in the late afternoon while a
succession of multicoloured birds came for titbits. There was the
red-breasted blackbird, the delicate blue-grey tanager, with its sky
blue feathers, the cheeky little yellow bananaquit, and sometimes
a small kiskadee. A white-lined tanager came, and a small greedy
green manakin with a parrot-shaped beak. There were wine-red
feathers, russet feathers and a little black bird who seemed to be
wearing wings made of Harris tweed.

One day we were sitting with our tea when a series of meows
rose from the direction of our neighbour's fence. I leapt up – 'Perhaps it's Squirrel!' – and went over to look. It wasn't Squirrel, but a
small tabby kitten with a pretty face, and a white front, walking up
and down on the other side, calling piteously. We put some food
on our side of the fence and settled down to wait. Sure enough,
there was a rustle in the purple bougainvillea and the little creature
dropped down, enticed by the saucer of chicken. When she had
eaten that, I replenished her bowl, a little closer this time, and she
ate that as well. Every night she came, just at nightfall, and the
bowl of food inched ever closer to where we were sitting. Closer
and closer she crept until she was eating at a distance of three metres. We began to see her more often during the day. She lost some
of her fear, and ventured into the kitchen. She came inside and ate

just inside the door. She even peeped through next door into the rest of the house, then turned tail and ran, appalled at her own temerity. The first time she was stroked, her whole body electrified with shock: 'Somebody touched me!'

Sometimes, wanting to make contact but not knowing how, she would make a soft-pawed swipe at a human foot or even take a small nip as we walked past. Finally one morning at breakfast time I bent down and picked her up. She was so surprised that she stayed where she was, and relaxed as her head was rubbed. After that she enjoyed being petted. She would wait for KJ outside his workshop and he would pick her up. When he put her down she would punish him by punching his ankles with her tiny soft paws – one, two; one, two! KJ put a small towel on a raised kitchen surface for her at night, so she could survey the scene and she was always there in the morning, ready for head-pushes. She investigated the TV room near the kitchen and ran in terror from the TV. Eventually she would sit on the settee between us watching the news, as she licked Marmite from a piece of toast.

'Pussycat' had been living on scraps from the dustbin next door. When the wire bin broke and was replaced there were no more scraps. Our little dustbin cat had been in danger of starvation. Only KJ and I could touch her. She ran away from the staff – particularly Beverley, who moved fast – and hid in the garden. But she would come when called and every night we had her company. She grew fat and happy.

Outside in the streets of Port of Spain there were so many stray dogs. They were gentle little things, in many shapes and sizes, often painfully thin. They ran in small packs, doing little harm but desperately searching for food. I carried ring-lock tins of dog or cat food in the boot of the car, together with some paper plates. When I saw a needy dog or two, it was easy to get out and give them a small meal. Better than nothing. One day, by the St Clair clinic, I saw a brown dog. He had been there for a while and I had time to stop. I got out, emptied a small can of cat food on to a paper plate and put it down for him. He was just about to eat when with a rush, a Rasta man complete with dreadlocks and red yellow and green knitted hat burst from the nearby bushes. He grabbed the paper plate, ravenously slurped up the cat food and ran away. I stood, shocked, with the spoon in my hand. How hungry must he have been! If I had known he was there I would have brought sandwiches. And the brown dog could have had his meal as well.

The year flew. Trinidadian festivals passed. National days took place with their colour and speeches. It would be our last Europe Day. Having taught the European anthem 'Ode to Joy' to a steel pannist last year, my ambitions this time stretched to a full choir. Enrique Ali, professional pianist and choir director, brought a quartet who sang it exquisitely in German and in the original soaring key. Each national day was different. For the Korean day delicate ladies came out like pastel coloured flowers in traditional Hanbok costumes. The Japanese national day was held at the embassy next door. Mieko and her ladies wore exquisite silk kimonos and served tempura straight from heaven. For 4th July, the American embassy arranged a Coca-Cola sponsorship and served tiny hamburgers. The Canadian embassy imported a famous band of girl folk singers to entertain the crowds. Sadly the noise level was so high that their song was reduced to opening and closing mouths. The Indian national day was held in the garden of the Indian residence, with coloured lights, tassa drums and spicy titbits served by ladies in rainbow saris. The Mexican national day was a lively one. Everyone who could wore some kind of Mexican national dress and beans in chocolate sauce were served. The enthusiastically patriotic Mexican ambassador dressed in peasant costume and waved the national flag violently as the operatic anthem was played.

Before we began on this diplomatic life I had held the fashionable liberal Western view that human beings are the same all over the world, and turned up my nose at the very idea of racial stereotyping. Even at HQ, it became obvious that this was not quite true. Traditional European traits did seem to apply, at times to a comical degree. KJ, with his linguistic gifts, found that, unconsciously, to get things done he would speak intellectually to French colleagues, logically to those from Germany, dramatically to the Italians and with full frontal directness to the Dutch.

As time went on, I began to realise that 'universal sameness' was a naïve generalisation. We are not the same. We have been brought up very differently. What is normal for me may be absolutely abnormal for you. I may bury my ancestors, you may reverently wash their bones every year or dance with their coffins. What makes me cry may make you laugh out loud. In southern Africa, an accident may be regarded as hilarious slapstick. I put ginger lilies in a vase and gaze at them – the Balinese chop them up as a spice. I like to have my colours gently co-ordinated. If you are from certain African nations, you may have a different arrangement of rods and cones in your eyes, and may see things differently, seeing beauty in bright colours that are splashy and clashing to others. I may love cats and dogs and monkeys as pets – perhaps you may eat them or sacrifice them to the gods. I came to realise that delight, fascination and wisdom come, not from pretending that difference do not exist, but from observing, recognising and understanding them and within that recognition, sharing all that we can. Wendy Fitzwilliam, a Trinidadian Miss Universe, put it well: 'Our differences should not divide but delight us!'

A Trinidadian friend of ours, Robin Montano, lawyer and sometime government minister dared to put this to the test. Robin was a tall handsome Trinidadian, urbane, sensitive and intelligent. He was also of a fearlessly experimental nature. He happened to be with the Chinese ambassador, a tall dignified and serious woman, at an evening function when something occurred to him. Turning to her he asked: 'What does English sound like to you?'

The ambassador, though she may well have understood English, employed a translator just to be on the safe side. Looking enquiring, she asked for the question to be repeated and the spectacled little translator did her best. The ambassador looked puzzled.

'Let me make myself clear!' said Robin, ploughing on dauntlessly. 'When I hear Chinese, the sound's something like this' – and he made a sort of strangled sing-song tonal noise, something like 'weow, weow, weow', up and down the scale. It was the sort of noise children might make when pretending to be Chinese. Sensing a potential international incident, we held our breath.

The Chinese ambassador began to laugh. She said something, and then made a noise.

'Now I see what you mean. This is what English sounds like' – and in her loudest gruffest voice she barked: 'Woof! Woof! Woof!'

As the year went on we knew we were coming to the end of our time overseas. In Suriname I had talked about 'waiting for the year 2001'. Now it was almost upon us. KJ was due to retire. His birthday was at the end of January, and he would have to be back at HQ to finalise everything before the clock struck, when he would fall off the computer system and all doors at HQ would close in his face. We decided to enjoy every minute that remained and, even better, to spend a truly Trinidadian Christmas.

November was upon us in no time and once more we were looking for sombre clothes to wear to the 11th November memorial service on the Savannah. It was a truly Trinidadian experience. Every year the pattern was the same. Early in the morning the mounted police rode past our front gate led by Winston, the beautiful Palomino. We knew they were coming when we heard the sound of horses' hooves on the road and the lances and pennants glided along the top of the garden wall. They would ride across the Wildflower Park, over the little bridge and culvert and disappear in the direction of the Savannah. Later on, appropriately dressed and hatted, we would arrive at the wooden platform where the yearly service would be held. The band would be drawn up in readiness to play. The mounted police would be standing at attention in their starched white uniforms, their immaculately groomed horses barely twitching a muscle. The representatives of all major religious groups would be sitting on their platform in full regalia, ready to take the microphone in a series of ecumenical readings and addresses. Children's choirs, hair brushed and plaited, eyes shining, were standing ready to sing. All was perfectly planned and in place.

And then, every year, inevitably, in the middle of the ceremony, it rained. Not a few drops, but strong, soaking tropical rain. Those of us with umbrellas put them up and only got wet around the edges. Others were not so lucky. The children would be soaked, singing with the water running down their little faces. The white starched uniforms of the mounted police were quickly drenched, limp and transparent. The horses' immaculate manes and tails were bedraggled. Programmes would be folded and used as rain hats. Proud old veterans sitting in their special chairs suddenly found that their legs were strong and the chairs much better used held over their heads as improvised roofs. The ceremony was cut short. Readings and speeches were curtailed. We all stood to attention as the twenty-one-gun salute was fired. As the guns boomed out every parrot in Trinidad took fright and flew squawking from the trees. The newest and least experienced of the horses flinched and jumped with each explosion, causing his rider to bounce up and down in a most undignified manner. And every multi-tonal car alarm for miles around went off, adding extra cacophony to this salute to the fallen.

Also in November came the President's Dinner. This was the glamorous event of the year. The entire corps was invited to President's House for a banquet. It was a black tie, full dress occasion with orchestra, choir and Christmas parang singing groups before the meal, floral arrangements, ice sculptures and waiters in white gloves. The much respected President Robinson always made a speech – without notes, since his now fading eyesight made it impossible for him to read.

One of the great pleasures of the year was deciding what to wear. For this year I had found a very special outfit indeed, a cream evening dress sewn with little seed pearls. Man-like, KJ announced that he might be in Curacao for a regional meeting and miss the dinner. Even he, a man, grasped the enormity of such a suggestion when I said with huge emphasis: 'But I've bought my dress!' Priorities are priorities, after all.

Ambassadors who lived in other Caribbean cities and were accredited to Trinidad and Tobago came for the occasion. Before dinner we spoke to the Norwegian ambassador, a serious lady of comfortable proportions who lived in Venezuela. Caracas is a city in a bowl of mountains and the airport sits at the foot of a mountain near the sea. The traffic at rush hour becomes completely clogged. Having sent her luggage on ahead, the Norwegian ambassador found herself stuck in the traffic, and about to miss her plane. She noticed a police motorcyclist on the verge monitoring traffic. Leaping from her official car, she ran to him and explained her predicament.

'Take me to the airport,' she said.

Hitching up her skirt, this apparently staid, dumpy and dignified lady hopped on to the back of the police motorbike, and together they roared to the airport, sirens howling as they wove through the traffic, just in time for the plane that would take her to the President's Dinner in Port of Spain.

As time went by, the diary began to get very crowded. There was the Caledonian Ball organised for charity by the British High Commission which involved more Scottish dancing classes and imported haggis. There were Christmas concerts by outstanding local choirs, a viewing of the new national airport, art exhibitions and KJ's own exhibition of his beautiful inlaid jewellery boxes to be held in the house. In the midst of it all, a mission from HQ announced its arrival to inspect a new road being built along the north coast of Tobago, linking east and west and opening up some hitherto deserted beaches. There were those who thought this was not a good thing. We decided to go and see.

Tobago is an island paradise, fringed with sandy beaches and palm trees, beloved of package tours and reputed to be the place where Robinson Crusoe landed. It has a predominantly Afro-Caribbean population, a relaxed, laid-back ambience and has, over the years, changed hands no less than twenty-two times, and been in fought over by the French, Dutch, British and Courlanders (Latvians).

The beaches on the northern coast are pristine, sheltered, peaceful and bucolic but with names like Bloody Bay, Man o' War Bay and Englishman's Bay. Together with the VIP from HQ we set out in a small hired four-wheel drive, ready for a rough ride on a road in the process of being constructed. There were two miscalculations. The first was that, unknown to us, it had been raining for the last week in Tobago and the new road was a sea of pale grey mud. The second was that we thought four-wheel-drive vehicles used all four wheels all of the time. The small carhire firm had omitted to explain that this little square vehicle had a setting on one of the wheels that needed to be turned before the pulling power came into force. We set off in good spirits, on the unmade roads, passing tractors and road-making machinery. As the road became rougher and the mud thicker we began to slide and stick. Finally, on a steep bank everything ground to a halt. KJ, the VIP and Luigi, the Italian engineering advisor, got out and began to push. All the usual techniques of logs, and hessian and branches were employed. Every time the engine was revved the men were spattered with whitish mud. Finally a local tractor was called and the car was hauled out. The Tobagonian driver leant down and looked at the gear on the front wheel. He turned it with a spanner.

'Now yeh fo' wheels workin'!' he said. It was a bit late.

We were towed to the nearest village. Families, children, and dogs came out to see the fun. All the men were wearing white mud boots up to the knees and were well whitewashed with splashes of earth. With great enthusiasm a hose was brought from a nearby house and the villagers set to work hosing down their visitors. The occasion turned to hilarity. Cold drinks were brought. As we sat, enjoying the atmosphere, a strange sight appeared at the top of the hill. A large strong woman in shorts was running hell for leather down the hill towards us together with a brown and white goat on a lead. She slowed down to talk. A German resident of Tobago, she was training every day for the Tobago goat races. Goat racing and crab racing are the national sports of Tobago but crabs, it seems, are more difficult to train.

At the beginning of December I realised that some clothes shopping would be needed. For twenty-two years, living and working in the tropics, my wardrobe had consisted of light summer clothes and sandals. A winter return to the UK loomed with its dread certainty of layers of dark heavy clothes and closed in boots. Any winter clothes still remaining had probably been hanging in a wardrobe in England for twenty years. If I were not to return looking like 'the lady from the colonies' something had to be done. Marie Sabga, my Lebanese neighbour, was going to Miami on a pre-Christmas shopping trip. Since American prices were half what would be charged in Britain I would go along.

We hit the shopping malls in Miami. There seemed to be no end to them. Marble columns stretched out before us, one arcade interlocking with another. We went from shop to shop, enjoying the Christmas excitement and the plethora of sales and bargains. Marie was a wise shopper and we found what we wanted. We also stopped at frequent intervals for coffee and refreshments, in an endless variety of American restaurants where one piled up plate of food would serve four normal people. We learned to order at most one dish for two, and ask for 'doggy bags'. I felt constantly stuffed.

Miami seemed to be manned exclusively by Spanish-speaking workers, often looking far from cheerful. In the malls, the bustling population was relentlessly driven, grimly shopping for more and more goods, more of the latest clothes to adorn themselves and more articles to have in their already full houses. No one smiled very much. The shoppers were either abnormally tanned, thin and athletic, or hugely obese – the latter clad in immense tracksuits and carrying along fistfuls of hamburgers, doughnuts or milk-shakes in case of starvation en route. There were other sights too. A great many middle-aged women appeared to have succumbed to facelifts, with unfortunate results. Expensively dressed and elegant, they wore tightly stretched faces and Chinese eyes, or strange ridges in their cheeks. Wrinkled necks and décolletage, and venerable be-ringed hands betrayed their age. Not good advertisements for their plastic surgeons. Strolling in the malls, too, were an extraordinary number of transvestites. Tall, statuesque men bore down on us, often in pairs, teetering on their size-ten stiletto heels, and carrying oversized handbags. Their faces, Dracula-like, were garishly made up with bright lipstick and thick black false eyelashes. It was like some Dantesque nightmare, a circle of hell where people were condemned to a desperate life of pretending to be what they were not.

One of the shops we had visited in Miami was 'The Christmas Shop' where, rather excessively, Christmas happened all the year – like eating chocolate for every meal. At least Christmas in Trinidad was in full swing only from the beginning of December though even that seemed a bit over the top. Beverley and Marisa had pleaded to put up the decorations early – 'So as to have a good long time to enjoy them.' But since I love Christmas too, for one last time, we went to town. Recklessly we linked in with the Trinidadian love for lights, tinsel, and poinsettia plants everywhere. The shops were full of cheap decorations. We had a Christmas tree trimmed with gold bows on the porch, icicle lights dripped from the eaves, Star's tree in the garden was an oasis of coloured lights and palm trees sparkled with white lights. The stairs were wound with green wreaths and twinkling lights. We raided the garden centre in Santa Cruz for poinsettia plants and put them everywhere we could. Beverley and Marisa were ecstatic, and, secretly, so was I.

We held a Christmas party. Beverley and Marisa enjoyed their work so much that Camille, Beverley's second daughter-in-law, pleaded to be allowed to join the team. A uniform was found for her and she came to help. With Living Water helping in the kitchen there were gales of laughter. Entertaining had changed over the years from a nail-biting ordeal to a creative game. Now it was a chance to experiment with things like plaited fish and striped soup. I had learned to play with the background music, just for fun, to see how it could instantly alter the mood of a gathering. Earlier in the year, Living Water had produced a new Italian menu and we had done a red, white and green party. Now, for Christmas we planned a gold and white dinner, with 'gold' platters, white and 'gold' table decorations, and little gold-wrapped presents for everyone.

Dr Harry Ramnarine held his annual Christmas party for friends. It was a wizard's Christmas party from *Harry Potter*. Harry presided. Instead of party games we chose cards that gave us a theme and direction for the next year. People sang and danced and said poems. I half expected the food to appear when he waved a wand over the table. Instead, equally magical spicy Indian dishes appeared, cooked with love by devoted clients.

We had a Lebanese Christmas Day next door with our neighbours, the Sabga family. Marie had been cooking and decorating for weeks. The Christmas tree with its opulent pink decorations was up. There was ham and turkey, and Lebanese delights, a magnificent construction of vine leaves arranged in geometric patterns, kibbe and Arabic rice, babaganouj, tabouleh, hummous and a giant red fish in tahini sauce. Desserts were served on tiered dishes. There were Lebanese sweetmeats – walnut and date ma'amoul and baklawah in all its forms, crunchy with pistachio nuts and juicy with honey. The Lebanese family were there, fifty-six of them, a self-sufficient social group, everyone excitedly interacting from great-grandmother down to the smallest new arrival. After lunch, carol-singing was de rigueur, a Trinidadian pianist came in to play, and Ramon, the paterfamilias, indulged his passion for singing like a Trinidadian Mario Lanza.

On Boxing Day it was Trinidad time. Friends went visiting or 'liming' from house to house, bringing small presents, and staying to drink sorrel or ponche crème, and eat Caribbean black cake, weaving home rather unsteadily after a day of reunions.

After the fireworks of New Year, it was time to think seriously about planning to leave. KJ had to be back at HQ to 'sign off' before the end of January. Life became a series of invitations to farewell dinners, presentations and sad goodbyes. The diary was black with events. KJ was rushing in and out, being farewelled by government departments. When he went to say goodbye to the president he wore, for the last time his 'going-to-the-president-suit'. To his secret delight he was escorted by mounted police into the President's House and played out by trumpeters, and the traffic lights around the Savannah were blocked so that the official car and its panoply of escorts could sail serenely back home.

The packers were coming. Those dreaded words. We had to clear out cupboards and tidy up. To cheer up the proceedings I had acquired from somewhere a selection of practical jokes. Every so often a sticky spider or a funny face would be introduced into the proceedings to stop us all from feeling too sad. The ladies joined in with gusto. One day Marisa concealed herself in the laundry basket and popped out like a jack-in-the-box as KJ came through the door. We were all appreciating each other and trying not to think of the end that was coming. Pussycat was found a home with a gentle lady who promised faithfully to take the greatest possible care of her. She was still nervous and semi-wild. There was no way she could have endured the journey to the UK. We sent her off with sadness and enough food for six months at least. We wished her a lovely life and completely entrusted her safety and happiness to her gentle new owner, knowing that she would be loved and guarded.

We were throwing one final farewell party for KJ's retirement and birthday combined. It was a chance to put into operation some long held fantasies. There was an old grapefruit tree in the garden. It had died during the year and we had planted a new one, but with its pure white trunk and branches the old tree was too beautiful to cut down. We decided it would be part of the party. Armed with poster paints from a toyshop, the staff and I climbed into the tree and painted it, blending the spectrum colours one into another so that it became a many-branched rainbow. I borrowed a fountain sprinkler for the pool and found a florist who could create floating flower arrangements on polystyrene platforms. Mr Kirwen de la Motte, electrician extraordinaire, outdid himself with spotlights on the rainbow tree and the floating flowers, we put little tea lights in all the hedges and wound lights around the palm tree trunks. We made flower arrangements for the many little tables in the garden and dotted them with candles. A friendly keyboard player even came along so that KJ could delight his fans with one last rendition of 'Danny Boy' as well.

After the party we sat round with the staff, filled with love and nostalgia, having our own little party and post mortem. Beverley and Marisa were there, Earl, Kirwen de la Motte, and the delightful bar staff who always came to help out. It felt like family.

The packers came, a gentle, quietly efficient team of old hands who were happy with all we had already done. One room after another was stripped bare and put into cardboard boxes and wardrobes. Beverley and Marisa's pile in the laundry grew steadily larger. The boxes and cases for Living Water's good causes piled high. I stood in the middle of the room trying to imagine what life would be like from now on. Would I ever again need china and cutlery for twenty-four people, twenty-seven decorative Zulu baskets, thirty-three cocktail dresses, twenty-five pairs of sparkly sandals, two silver tea sets and a partridge in a pear tree? Had I ever truly needed them? The house was becoming steadily emptier. After the packing cases were put into their container and taken away, we were left with memories, a sinking feeling, and a container padlock key in our hand.

All possessions having gone, the farewells and gifts went on. On the penultimate day we were in the house, clearing and tidying and trying to fit everything into the suitcases we had reserved. Leandra, our bubbly Trinidadian lawyer friend, arrived, bringing a box of beautiful biscuits from a patisserie. When I thanked her she said: 'Oh, these aren't for you.' I looked surprised. 'No,' she said, 'these are for all the people who will be coming to see you tomorrow.' I must have looked horrified. 'Don't you know?' she said. 'Everyone will come around on the last day to say goodbye. You'll need something to give them.'

And so it was. From breakfast time on the last day the telephone began ringing and the gate bell sounded. People phoned and visited non-stop. In our usual fashion we were packing for that night's plane. Everyone who came was a loving friend and we wanted to talk to them all. Everyone who came brought a present. We were inundated with every conceivable object in the shape of steel pans, red ibis, hummingbird and the Trinidadian map and flag. We were even given a long black velvet banner called 'Memories of Trinidad' which was painted with all of them together. Every time we saw someone approaching with yet another parcel we inwardly groaned. Our relaxed young artist friend Vanessa came in the middle of the afternoon. When KJ said we had to pack she said: 'Oh, that doesn't matter, I'll sit on the bed and watch you!' And she did.

Suddenly I became aware that the phone hadn't rung for the last hour. 'No, it hasn't,' said KJ. 'I took it off the hook.' And of course then I felt guilty in case some other friends had been trying to get through.

We ran out of packing space. We had, that morning, returned a red suitcase to Marie next door, and had to phone her to borrow it right back again.

Finally we thought it was all done. There was half an hour to go before catching the plane to Tobago. There was a ring at the front gate. Mr and Mrs Kirwen de la Motte had arrived carrying a parcel that was all of two feet square. It was a parcel of freshly made roti – small spicy curry puffs, still hot, in case there was nothing good to eat on the plane. We thanked her effusively but we were seriously spatially challenged.

Earl arrived to take us to the airport. We hugged everyone hard, already feeling bereft. Having been a part of this place, this life, for only three years, once again we had given our hearts and were being torn away. As the car swept along the highway we looked at this beloved island and wondered when we would see it again.

We were staying for two nights in Tobago, to recover. There was a jacuzzi on the balcony of the hotel room. We went out wrapped in towels, and closed the glass door to preserve the air conditioning. Having filled the tub we lay in it, blissfully de-stressing. When we got out to go back inside there was no way back into the room. The glass door had sealed itself. We were stranded naked on a first-floor balcony. We looked out into the gardens but there was no one to call. The phones were inside the room. Only after half an hour of scratching, probing, leaning and pushing did the door consent to open again.

Early the next morning I woke up with a start. I had distinctly heard the sound of the gate closing at Number Eight Prada Street, Port of Spain, I had heard Pussycat meow and had felt the swing and sway of my car going round the Savannah. Such beautiful, yearning, painful nostalgia.

We went down to breakfast. To our astonishment, Prime Minister Basdeo Panday and his entire Cabinet were there for a meeting. KJ rallied. He went over to shake hands, grinning broadly and saying: 'How good of you gentlemen to come over to say farewell, but it really wasn't necessary.'

As we set foot on the gangway of the plane we felt the warm, caressing air of the tropics. It would be the last time we would feel this warmth for a long, long time. What would life be like from now on? We had no idea. We only knew that we were returning to a different Europe from the one we had left and that we too were very different from the two young people who had landed in Johannesburg on our first assignment twenty-two years earlier.

Postscript
What was it all about?

This life in diplomacy has been a life of excitement, happiness, friendship, challenges, discoveries, contrasts, luxury, discomfort and sometimes loneliness. There have been times of tears and times of wonder. Over the years we have lost any concept of 'home' we may once have had – I no longer use the word – but in return we have had a life of kaleidoscopic change. Few of us who live and work in countries other than our own really appreciate the treasures that we are given – often we are just too busy or stressed coping with the changes and the demands of each moment. Sometimes we are depressed or irritated. All too often we spend precious time hankering after the imagined humdrum comforts of 'home' when the present moment is offering us precious experience and vivid human contacts that will never come again.

It is only in retrospect, savouring those years, that we realise what treasure we have been given. Every chance to experience other worlds, other lives and other visions is a cause for gratitude. It is like being given a telescope that magnifies life. In adjusting to other climates, other ways of living and other life views, we learn our own strengths and weaknesses and we come into contact with all the resourcefulness and strength that exist in people wherever we are. Even the most diminishing events are, in the end, an expansion.

Because of the nature of the job, we hope to have represented genuine and good European ideals. We hope to have left behind official relationships that are warmer and more understanding. We hope to have left behind some people whose lives are a little easier, who have schools, roads, bridges, hospitals and better health. But as we go, like rolling snowballs, we receive so much. We gather friends in every country, from every walk of life. We are privileged to receive far more than we give.

Then one day, quite suddenly, it is all over. We 'retire' – whatever that may mean – back to a land that is no longer our true 'home' bringing with us a rich global net of memories and friendships, carrying in our hearts with so much love and thankfulness all of those beloved scenes, events and people, whose particular dearness was associated with a particular age, place and time, and which will never be known in quite that way again.

As John O'Donohue says:

> *There is a place where our vanished days secretly gather,*
> *And the name of that place – is Memory.*